The Management of Change

Multilingual Matters

Please contact us for the latest book information:
Multilingual Matters,
Bank House, 8a Hill Rd,
Clevedon, Avon BS21 7HH,
England

BERA Dialogues 1

The Management of Change:

Increasing school effectiveness and facilitating staff development through action research

Edited by

Pamela Lomax

MULTILINGUAL MATTERS LTD
Clevedon ● Philadelphia

Library of Congress Cataloging-in-Publication Data

The management of change : increasing school effectiveness and
   facilitating staff development through action research / edited by
   Pamela Lomax.
      p. cm. — (BERA dialogues ; 1)
      Bibliography: p.
      Includes index.
      1.Action research in education.   2. Teaching.   3. Teachers—In-
service training.   I. Lomax, Pamela, 1941– . II. Series.
LB1028.24.M36   1989   89-9228
371.1—dc20   CIP

British Library Cataloguing in Publication Data

The management of change.—(BERA dialogues; 1).
   1. Schools. Administration. Theories
   I. Lomax, P. (Pamela)   II. Series
   371.2′001

   ISBN 1-85359-061-4
   ISBN 1-85359-060-6 pbk

Multilingual Matters Ltd

Bank House, 8a Hill Road   &   242 Cherry Street
Clevedon, Avon BS21 7HH   Philadelphia, Pa 19106–1906
England   USA

Typeset by Proteus, Worle, Avon
Printed and bound in Great Britain by Short Run Press Ltd., Exeter EX2 7LW.

Contents

1 The management of change through action research: an introduction

LINDA BANNISTER, PAMELA LOMAX and
JACK WHITEHEAD

The form of the collaboration that resulted in this introduction was a dialogue; a conversation that we taped. It was difficult to transcribe the quality of this encounter; to indicate the importance of those fundamental feelings and nonverbal signals that enlivened the meeting and gave its outcome its richness and value. This is a problem that we have to take on board as educational action researchers: the problem of using those performance indicators that we believe are relevant to demonstrating educationally valid change and improvement.

The style of this book is unusual for a book about research. Its fundamental premise is that education is about values and that all research acts within education should include an examination and a refinement of these values and an attempt to make them central to practice. Values are problematic for us; they tend to be unquestioned in traditional research. Another reason why the style of the book is unusual for a book about research is that we are all teachers and have all had experience in schools. The research presented is teacher research. We have used narrative or dialogue and sometimes poetry in order to retain the richness of the practices and values described: this is different from the way in which research is normally presented. We think it is less elitist and more accessible. We have treated our work as art and painted our pictures accordingly.

In the first chapter Mary Gurney makes the point that the finely developed styles of communicating research used in education perpetuate restricted practices and exclude many people from sharing its insights. We do not intend to fall into that trap. One of the purposes of coming together to produce this collection of case studies about managing change is to share our educational values and practices with a much wider band of accomplices, namely other teachers who care about improving the quality of education for their pupils. We see ourselves as a critical community of researchers, engaging in a living form of educational theory and reaffirming this through dialogue. It seems fitting that we will be the first authors in the new (and hopefully influential) series of occasional publications from BERA (British Educational Research Association), aptly named Dialogues.

In an earlier paper the notion of a documentary was used to describe the way in which members of a critical community could engage with each other in a continuing definition of their theory, practice and research for improving education (Lomax, 1986a). The idea was that such a community would not allow their living form of educational work to be appropriated by *experts* and by *expert* definitions of what would constitute action research. The documentary, as metaphor for the work of this community, was to be ongoing and open. Those who participated might take any or all of the possible roles — director, camera person, actress and actor, scriptwriter — the important thing being that the documentary would remain open to interpretation by the owner-participants. This is the theory and practice of action research.

This book is part of the history of the documentary. It contains a collection of narratives about action research. All the narrators are telling their own story. Although all the authors are teachers and they are all describing their own educational practices, they represent the sweep of our educational institutions; they come from the infant school, the special school, the secondary modern school, the comprehensive school, the college of higher education, the polytechnic and the university.

In the first part of the book the narratives focus on the research method. They clarify what action research is about; why it is the most effective form of research for both school teachers and college lecturers; how it can be integrated into an individual's continuing professional development; and how the action researcher gets started. Three of the contributors to Part I are from schools and they offer evidence of school teachers' acceptance of the *relevance* of action research to their work.

Both Mary Gurney and Barrie Jones set the context of action research by arguing a case for the relevance of action research to their work as practising teachers. Both of them have tried traditional research but found that it did not inspire them to use it as a basis for improving their own practices. Mary argues from the perspective of the classroom teacher, and the experience of being on the receiving end of how *experts outside the classroom* defined *her* classroom realities. Barrie argues from the perspective of the college lecturer who found himself preaching a research gospel that he did not practise himself. Both claim that action research has changed their view of the place of research in enabling professional development.

Mary's chapter describes part of an action research project in which she set about improving personal and social education. At the heart of her project was the desire to involve pupils in the evaluation and improvement of their own learning. To do this it became necessary to work with colleagues in the school and with other teachers as part of a school-based in-service programme. It is not surprising to read between the lines of the paper and find conflict. She writes: 'action research implies change and change can be very threatening . . .'. For Mary, action research provided a way of stepping aside from personal attacks made on her work, so that she could deal with the problems. In other circumstances she might have abandoned her in-service work in the face of what seemed considerable opposition. Action research enabled her to cope with the difficulties.

Mary sets a challenge for teachers by arguing that improving education is their right, not an activity that belongs to academics, and that they should assert this right. Her message comes clearly from the title of her chapter: in the past teachers have been implementors of other folk's ideas; with action research they should be innovators. In using terms like 'professional improvement' rather than 'professional development', she brings a ring of truth to those classic teacher arguments for the relevance of focusing on their own classroom practices. The result of reading this chapter should be to fire teachers' enthusiasm for action research. The thought of change growing outwards from individual classrooms, and of *communities of enquirers* committed to democratic forms of educational management, should prove to be irresistible to some teachers.

It could be argued that at times Mary presents a somewhat pessimistic view of teachers' abilities to reflect and communicate; also her explanation of why teachers do not use research sounds more forceful than her account of how the situation could be improved. Neither of these outcomes are intended and she would point to her own massive case study of the development of personal and social education to refute such criticism (Gurney, 1988).

David Forward wrote his chapter in the context of a project in which he developed and implemented form-based pastoral programmes in a secondary school. It took him over six years to bring about this massive organisational change: two years reconnaisance, three years' implementation and then evaluation and writing up the case study. As with Mary, what started as a curriculum change became a massive staff development exercise. It is not surprising that working within the action research paradigm for such a long time enables the researcher to express so clearly the principles that have guided the work. There are several interesting aspects to David's account. It is a usable account of action research, full of hints for the new action researcher. There is a fascinating insight into the difficulty of giving up ownership of the project once other staff have become involved and are willing to move the innovation forward. There is also some interesting comment about the effect that being promoted has on the action researcher's role within the school.

The disjunction between the theory and practice of education is at the centre of educational action research. The living contradiction that we experience ourselves to be when we deny our values in our practice is a starting point for action — the beginning of that cycle of reflection, action and evaluation so dear to us action researchers (Whitehead, 1977, 1980a). Andy Larter and Barrie Jones approach the problem of the dialectic in action research from two different perspectives. Andy's is a philosophical approach, in which he draws heavily on insights gained from careful reading and uses them as a basis for reflection on his own practice. His writing is in the form of a dialogue where he uses the texts of others to engage himself in question and answer in order to explore the contradictions of his theory and practice as a secondary school English teacher.

Barrie uses a similar dialogic style, but his approach is literary and poetic rather than philosophical — allowing the reader to experience a certain delight in relation to the language used. His account describes his conversion to action research with an openness and honesty rarely found in writings about research. The other in Barrie's dialogue is the voice of his conscience rather than that of his philosopher friends. The function of this other is similar to that of Andy's other — it is to explore the dilemmas of theory and practice, values and action and to work towards a negation of the negation.

The second part of the book clearly places action research in the classroom and the school, and highlights its benefits for practising teachers; both for their own professional development and also for the development of other staff and for the school as a whole. These narratives describe claims that teachers have made about improving their own practice and provide evidence to support these claims, so that you, the reader, can be part of the validation process. This work is something to which many teachers will respond, some teachers will act upon, and a few will criticise as anecdotal. Few readers will question the authenticity of these accounts and those who do will not be teachers. These accounts show that many of the outcomes of action research are unexpected and often move in directions that were not anticipated. The three narratives describe action research in a special school, in an open plan infant school, and in a secondary school. Kate Burton's work focuses on the management role, Margaret Follows' on a bottom-up model of whole school change and Rod Linter's on the classroom.

Kate Burton's chapter highlights the transformation which can be brought about by action research in an individual's and an institution's practice. Part of the work is about using action research to help her reflect upon and change her own particular style of management. Part of it is about the way in which she set about reducing sexism in the school where she had been newly appointed deputy headteacher. The strength and support of the action research paradigm is clear in her account. Kate was in a situation where she encountered attitudes which strongly contradicted her own values, and action research enabled her to step aside from personal response. As with the case of Mary Gurney, she could tackle the problem of opposition, through using the discipline of the action research cycle of enquiry, action and reflection. The model has the effect of strengthening resolve and diverting the more usual personalised way of responding to difficulties.

Margaret Follows provides an account of how she set up a collaboration to bring about co-operative teaching in a semi-open plan infant school. Her chapter will appeal to readers who have experienced the realities of the open plan infant school, and are aware of the divide that often exists between the theory and practice of open plan provision. Margaret's account demonstrates the skill with which an action researcher is able to involve her collaborators to the extent that they become committed participants in the improvements being sought. Her chapter will be extremely useful to anyone interested in strategies for staff development that enable a school staff to become a self-critical community working towards a whole school policy for change.

Rod Linter's chapter is about how he engaged his fourth-year sociology class more actively in their own learning; and how this led to the discovery that girls were being disadvantaged in the learning process. Of particular interest in this account is the way in which he draws pupils into the action research by getting them to reflect his practice back to him. Not only do they become collaborators, giving feedback about the processes of learning that he initiates; they become action researchers using self-reflection to understand their own part in the learning process. Like Margaret Follows, Rod persuades colleagues to act as collaborators. They sit in the back of his classroom and record interactions; they help him make sense of the video recordings that he makes of his lessons; they allow him to sit in on their lessons to find out if pupils behave in other classes as they do in his. In the end he draws them into the research so that they become more than collaborators and the scene is set for the action research to move from his classroom to department level.

In the last part of the book the narrators are people who stand on the outside of classrooms but whose job is to support and help those within them. Some critics question whether action research is an appropriate paradigm for the outsider to adopt. What conclusions can be drawn? Can they be more than abstract generalisations about teachers' theories and practice that help to illuminate events for teachers but cannot really alter their practice or improve their situation?

In the first chapter in Part III Pamela Lomax talks about the relationship between evaluation, course development and action research. She approaches the dilemma of the outsider by emphasising her role as collaborator and critical friend who supports the action research of teachers but herself uses the discipline of action research to improve the quality of that support she is giving. She argues that this is the key to action research; that whatever form collaboration takes, the action researcher must reflect critically on her own part in that collaboration. Pamela talks about a particular programme of management training in which the action research model is internal to the structure of the course, influencing the way in which it develops and changes through formative evaluation at both personal and institutional levels. This has parallels for the evaluation of classroom work and the assessment of pupils' learning with strong implications for the involvement of pupils in the evaluation and improvement of their own learning.

The second chapter was written at a distance and demonstrates how an outsider (John Cowan) can help the action researcher (Pamela Lomax) reflect critically on her own practice. It is interesting because of the *distance learning* aspect of the strategy. It is also interesting because of the way in which the outside collaborator becomes embroiled in examining his own practice. This tells us a number of things about the way in which collaboration moves people into the participation mode. At the end of the exercise John had this to say about the experience of collaborative writing:

> It strikes me that the dialogue swings in a very interesting way. In the beginning, and for quite some time, you use my comments as a foil to bring out points which you appear to wish to make. Then, just as it would appear that this guy John is a stooge, I burst out with a number of strong arguments to which it seemed to me you were making very profound responses. I remember you asked me early on if I thought the style fruitful. I confess that, while I was taking part in it, I could not see it producing anything readable and useful. Now that I see the end result, I have a very different view.

In the third chapter Pat Broadhead describes her role as an outsider facilitating primary school teachers' understanding and improvement of their own practice. She recognises that her own research is very different from teacher-action research, the research being in the hands of the outsider. Yet what she has attempted to do is to address those tensions as a positive basis for action within the partnership; and she has used the action research tools of critical self-reflection on her own role in the process. She feels it important to address and explore the form such partnerships might fruitfully take if teachers' theoretical constructs are to be recognised as crucial contributors to deeper understanding of teaching and learning.

It is clear that her reflections on the insider/outsider dichotomy of role are relevant to any INSET (In-service education and training of teachers) development, even teacher-led school-based in-service work. There are stages of being an outsider — we are outsiders in our colleagues' classrooms, so even if we work in the same school, we still experience the outsider dilemma. Action research can render this boundary or division harmless, if, in implementing the model, we work from the premise of what each can contribute. Emphasis on collaboration, with mutual respect for the different contributions and perspectives of participants, enriches exchanges and blurs barriers. In seeing things from the other's position it is possible to break out from the self-sufficiency competency model and grow.

Pat believes that action research has to seek wider recognition of its value as a tool for learning and as a valid contributor to theory building and sharing amongst teachers. She argues that insiders and outsiders can no longer accept the inevitability of divergent perspectives; they must both actively seek common ground. Neither must be perceived as owning the prerogative of the first initiative. Both should feel empowered to initiate and should see the value of the other as an equally weighted contributor. There are implications in this work for staff development in schools and a good role model to which advisers and inspectors of schools might aspire.

The idea that teachers have implicit theories about their work in classrooms is not new. Neither is the belief that they have difficulty making these theories explicit. On the one hand it is argued that teaching is based on a sense of form that cannot be fully articulated, and on the other that the articulate teacher is the true extended professional (Lomax, 1987). Hugh Busher addresses this issue by suggesting that in their everyday work teachers do not need to articulate their theories fully, though they can do so when asked to. In his account of one inexperienced teacher reflecting on her practice he shows somebody struggling to explicate for a puzzled outsider practices which she lives as commonplace. His paper focuses on how a teacher has learnt to adapt her practices to fit with the demands of her school. He suggests that stimulated recall and discussion with the aid of a video record in the company of a critical friend enable a teacher to make public her taken-for-granted classroom practice, and so to reflect on her actions about her classroom practice.

This is an exciting addition to our portfolio of techniques for enabling critical reflection but it has many pitfalls which Hugh recognises in his chapter. His own position as an outsider in this scenario is problematic. He acknowledges that there is the dilemma of the non-participant observer: how far does he distort the situation; how far can intervention aid the reflection process and how far does it influence in directions preferred by the outsider? As well as trying to help the insider reflect on her situation, the outsider is forced to reflect on his own practice and on his understanding of the insider's situation. In being a critical friend he becomes an insider with the teacher with respect to the situation in their discussions.

Hugh's attempts to help a teacher articulate her own theories about her practice became problematic as he found he had to provide a logical framework to make sense of her talk. It is difficult to tell how far he was controlling the teacher's meanings about her practice by this framework. We all are susceptible to this problem. In our enthusiasm to make sense of others' actions we impose our own meaning. Hugh's work has important implications for appraisal work in schools because of both the pitfalls that he identifies and the techniques that he uses. It certainly could provide a useful model for working with individual teachers who wish to enhance their professionality.

The part played by colleges and the in-service educational support that they provide shines through all the accounts of action research presented in this book. College-based in-service provision was the incentive for the start of all the action enquiry described here. The question we must address is that of how far this mode of professional development will continue after the support of the college has ended. There is the danger that when a particular college course is completed and the teacher no longer has the support of tutors and colleagues on the course, other things will take over and the action enquiry mode will be pushed aside. It is also possible to envisage constraints that are too overwhelming for individuals or small groups of teachers to combat without external support. Despite these pressures we are optimistic and think there is quite substantial evidence that action enquiry becomes self-generating. Often there is a gap between the end of one programme and the start of another. Perhaps it is the intensity of action enquiry that demands that the researcher takes time out to reflect in the light of experience and refine ideas before starting again.

This seems to have been the experience in Avon, where groups of up to six teachers in each of 10 schools engaged in an action research enquiry to bring about an active curriculum in relation to TVEI (Technical and Vocational Educational Initiative). After one year the funding for the TRIST (Teacher Related In-Service Training) project ended. The authority then funded a programme of support for teachers in their classroom action enquiries as part of the Avon curriculum review and evaluation programme for 1987/88. Jack Whitehead was engaged as a consultant to support this work. The working papers produced from this programme were published by the authority for internal use by Avon teachers; they are now being used in an extended programme of support for classroom action enquiries in the 1988/89 session. Their value is that they show what needs to be strengthened in the current enquiries. For example, an emphasis is now being given to gathering evidence which will enable the group to make evaluative judgements on the quality of pupils' learning, a key area in the present drive to increase school effectiveness.

One interesting feature of the teachers' work was the tendency to take on too much in the first year of the enquiry, then to disengage for the second year, before reformulating a more manageable project in the third year. The groups which disengaged provided places for new groups. Each year the available funding has increased, enabling most needs to be met. How the network will adapt to local management of schools remains to be seen.

Where action research is self-generating, where it continues in a school or starts up again after a dormant period, there is the danger that it will not be made public. Teachers are not very good at publicising their work, though things may change with the new forms of competition being encouraged between schools. Avon have published a newsletter, *Learning Matters*, whose purpose is to publicise such initiatives and to keep teachers informed about what is going on in the authority's schools. We believe that publications like BERA Dialogues for a national audience and *Learning Matters* for a local audience, will provide a forum in which important educational developments can be debated, made public and used to inform local and national policy and decision making about education.

Part I:
Action research for all

2 Implementor or innovator? A teacher's challenge to the restrictive paradigm of traditional research

MARY GURNEY

This chapter is concerned with both curriculum and professional development. There is a limited number of ways in which teachers can extend their professional development beyond the levels of improvement associated with increased experience. I believe that teachers do not readily look to the resources of research to inform and improve their practice. The dominant approach to professional improvement is through in-service training courses. I have pursued curriculum and professional development through a regionally organised in-service training course, as well as a range of locally organised courses. The in-service input to my work led to improvement in my practice but it also led to recognition of the need for an additional and different approach to curriculum innovation. The possibility of pursuing a research study as a different approach to curriculum development was not an immediately obvious option.

Before I give my reasons for choosing research as a method of tackling the curriculum problems which have arisen in the development of personal and social education and as a method for developing understanding of the learning process, I will look at the way in which research is viewed by teachers. I will then consider some of the advantages of research and in so doing I will be making out a case for regarding research as a basis for teaching and for professional development. The justification for the choice of a particular research paradigm, namely action research, and for the claim that this form of research is a powerful basis for teaching will also be covered.

For reasons of clarity I will use the term 'teacher' to refer to a school-based teacher and the term 'academic' to refer to a university- or college-based teacher; I have no wish to perpetuate any divide between the two bodies of the same profession. I accept and use the definition of research which Stenhouse (1981a) has given us. He took as a minimal definition 'systematic enquiry made public' and elaborated upon this to define research as

> systematic and sustained enquiry, planned and self-critical, which is subjected to public criticism and to empirical tests where these are appropriate. Where empirical tests are not appropriate, critical discourse will appeal to judgement of evidence — the test, the document, the observation, the record.

There is a widespread view among many teachers that research has little relevance to everyday practice. The production and distribution of research knowledge is seen by teachers as the domain of academics in universities and colleges, and there is certainly a dearth of practising teachers engaged in education research. Rudduck (1985) recognises 'a pattern of inequality in relation to teachers and research'; and Nixon (1981), writing as a teacher-researcher keen to see research 'initiated, conducted and disseminated from inside the classroom', reports that the traditional view of educational research is 'activity indulged in by those *outside* the classroom for the benefit of those *outside* the classroom'. The right to engage in educational research seems to be firmly located on the side of the academics, though they may well have a more positive view about the usefulness of their work than Nixon suggests. It is up to teachers to challenge the view that research is the prerogative of academics and demonstrate the value of research conducted from within the classroom. We must show that 'participant' or 'interpretative research which takes actors' (research subjects) accounts as valid descriptions and provides the basis for a rich description of practice and events' (Adelman & Young, 1985) can not only make a significant contribution to improving the quality of learning in our classrooms but can also inform or extend public debate on educational issues. Research, as Mitchell (1985) suggests, should be the basis of a partnership between schools and institutions of higher education.

So long as we accept the dominant view of research, as the work conducted by academics, we will remain locked in our somewhat insular and parochial attitude towards professional development. We should take up the theme of 'emancipation', which Jean Rudduck and David Hopkins believe is the central concept of the work of Lawrence Stenhouse (Rudduck & Hopkins, 1985). In a lecture to the Dartington conference in 1978 Stenhouse gave his view that the 'essence of emancipation . . . is the autonomy which we recognize when we eschew paternalism and the role of authority and hold ourselves obliged to appeal to judgement' (Stenhouse, 1978). There is a need for radical change in our approach to professional development. As teachers we need to be much more positive and creative in our outlook towards professional development and assert our rights to be involved in improving education. I do not agree entirely with Hutchinson & Whitehouse (1986) when they say that teachers uncritically accept the social reality in which they are immersed and in which certain role-models are presupposed. Many of us are critical of our reality but we are not empowered to do anything to change matters. This leads to a good deal of frustration and conflict, as we experience contradiction between our values and social reality. We will not improve the quality of our practice if we are passive to these contradictions or if we accept that external authority can entirely dictate the course of curriculum development. Unfortunately teachers seem to have very little say in decisions relating to major educational change; never has this issue been so critical as at the present time of the Education Reform Bill. At a time when the collective energies of teachers have been exhausted by action surrounding pay and conditions, when we are immersed, not feeling properly prepared, in major examination reform, the timing of further and controversial reform has ensured that the effect of critical debate is minimalised. As Sir Peter Newsam writes in the *Guardian* (2.3.88), the 'effort involved in responding to the consultative process tends to exhaust, as it has done on this occasion, those who take part in it'. I found that the printed acknowledgement of receipt of my response to the national curriculum proposals, indicating that the points made will not be acknowledged in a meaningful way, created in me a feeling of futility.

I see that what is urgently required is dialogue between authority and practitioners, between school and society, between parents and teachers, between teachers and academics, so that we may develop meaningful objectives which can be subjected to the critical judgement of all those interested in the education of our young people. I realise that there is some truth in Tyrell Burgess' observation that 'schools themselves seldom have any clear objectives of their own and so far as they have any, these objectives are not what society attributes to them' (Burgess, 1973). However, to overcome this historical legacy, teachers need to be encouraged to move out of their submissive position and to take a much more innovatory, as opposed to implementary, role in curriculum development. One way to do this is to adopt the perspective of researcher, since educational enquiry is a vital way in which we can improve our understanding of teaching and learning and thereby may improve our practice.

The argument for teachers adopting the dual role of teacher-researcher has been made most persuasively by Stenhouse (1975, 1979, 1981a, 1981b), Rudduck (1985), Elliott & Adelman (1973a, 1973b), Nixon (1981), Hopkins (1985) and Whitehead (1983a, 1983b, 1986). Rudduck & Hopkins (1985) rest their argument for research as a basis for teaching on two principles:

first, that teacher research is linked to the strengthening of teacher judgement and consequently to the self-directed improvement of practice; second, that the most important focus for research is the curriculum in that it is the medium through which knowledge is communicated in schools.

McCutcheon (1981) has outlined the advantages of the teacher in the researcher role. The teacher's role permits a view of practice from the insider's perspective. Through research, teachers are able to share their view of their classroom life with others. Teachers are in a position to carry out long-term studies of classroom practice, with a high degree of continuity. A teacher engaged in research has the opportunity to pose questions which are relevant to his practice, and seek ways of understanding and improving his own situation. Through research, teachers may contribute to the community of discourse, taking a more active part in determining the path of curriculum development.

There are a range of attitudes which impede such development, and I can report on some of these from the teacher's perspective. For many, research by teachers is regarded as flight of fancy for the ambitious or dedicated few who do not have enough work to do. Sometimes research is seen as a means of temporary escape from the classroom and a way of bettering one's qualifications. It is certainly not seen as a valid means of professional development nor as a means of improving the quality of teaching, nor a basis for curriculum development. In spite of the efforts of the Schools Council Programme Two (Elliott, 1981) to promote teacher research as a means of professional development, research has not become a widely accepted approach to professional development and curriculum improvement. One of the principles of the Schools Council Programme Two was that classroom research undertaken by teachers on problems they have helped to identify, is an effective strategy for promoting curriculum development. The Programme emphasised that teachers' professional development is an integral part of curriculum development and that research by teachers enhances professional effectiveness. There are a few authorities, such as Avon, Cambridgeshire and Sheffield, that have recognised the value of teacher research, and networks of teacher-researchers are growing up in these areas.

If there is any divide between teachers and academics on the right to pursue research, we must take our share of blame. Similarly, if my authority does not push for more research by teachers it may be because we have not expressed much interest or desire to engage in such activity. This may be partly due to the fact that we have found that much educational research seems to express itself in findings which do not offer us much scope for action in our classroom settings. We see experimental and analytical research attempting to form generalisations which do not apply to our situation. Burgess (1980) has commented on teachers' attitudes towards research:

> They [teachers] consider that much educational research has little relevance for the work they do in schools and classrooms. Second, they consider that research reports are relatively inaccessible, given their content and style of presentation. Thirdly, they feel that many researchers exploit schools for their own purposes but provide little evidence that will influence classroom practice.

As Stenhouse (1975) asserts, 'it is not enough that teachers' work should be studied: they need to study it for themselves'. What we need is a different view of research which begins with our own work and which is 'founded in curiosity and a desire to understand; which is a stable, not fleeting, curiosity, systematic in the sense of being sustained by a strategy' (Stenhouse, 1981a). We need to change our attitude concerning what counts as research and look for opportunities to engage in research which will communicate itself to other practitioners.

I recognise that we are often not very good at reflecting on what we do nor at explaining why we do things, and thus we do not tend to produce a well-articulated epistemology and rationale for our work. Though we may be very good practitioners we do not think others will take us seriously, for we have nothing profound to say. Profundity is for those with the gift of rhetoric and time to study. We mistakenly believe that research has to be either controversial or far-reaching in its observations but, equally, we are fairly unimpressed by small-scale study which tells us what we sensed or knew anyway. By and large, research is not common practice amongst us and we take little or no notice of the research of others. I was as guilty of this as any other teacher until Rutter published his study of ethos in schools (Rutter *et al.*, 1979). This study broke through the barrier of my 'typical teacher' resistance to, or unawareness of, ongoing research relevant to my work and interests. I feel sure that some of the reasons for this research having impact are due to its popular-style publication, easily understood language and appeal to commonsense; in other words, what Rutter had found seemed to have direct relevance to what was going on in schools, to everyday practice and concerns. Rutter and his team had tackled an enormous issue in schools, that of the impact of school ethos, and though there may be some criticism of technique, the ground covered contributed a great deal to the debate inside school about what we were doing. I think it also helped that members of the research team went out to teachers to discuss their findings with them, and the opportunity to attend an open meeting with Janet Ouston (at Bristol University in 1979) helped me to realise some of the values of research and started me thinking about the potential usefulness of research findings. However, I still had not thought about the benefits of actually engaging in research as a practising teacher. My view of professional development was through the in-service training provision, with courses provided by the 'experts' who then left us to make what we could, or could not, of the wisdoms we gleaned through this model.

The problem of our lack of self-image with regard to whether or not we have anything of value to contribute to the body of educational knowledge and understanding, is certainly a stumbling block in our development. We do not speak the 'conventional language of research reportage' (Rudduck, 1985) and, besides inhibiting us, this reinforces our inferior position in relation to research. Walker (1986) has examined the implications of existing systems of research reporting, in his article 'Breaking the grip of print'. He holds the view that the finely developed styles of comunicating research, as used in education, perpetuate restricted practice and exclude any change in approach. This amounts to a subtle form of control over participation: 'The language of curriculum research adds to the accretion of established structures, reinforcing attitudes, values and practices and legitimising the existing distribution of information and access to knowledge' (Walker, 1986).

An additional disadvantage is that we have not received training in research techniques, particularly in our initial training. 'The development of research skills is basically dependent on the opportunity to exercise the research function' (Barnes, 1960); and since mostly we are not involved in this mode of development, there is little point in learning skills which will not be used. In addition, as Nixon (1981) says in *A Teachers' Guide to Action Research*, one of the blocks to the development of action research in schools is the lack of information concerning the range of research techniques available for use in the classroom. Many teachers, if they think of educational research at all, see it within a narrow tradition of psychometric testing and statistical analysis.

A further aspect of the way in which we see ourselves in relation to research is reflected in the dichotomy mentioned earlier, between the two roles of implementor and innovator. It seems to me that we tend to be content to see ourselves as 'knowledge appliers' rather than 'knowledge generators' — a distinction used by Elliott & Ebbutt (1984) in looking at different forms of professional development. They indicate the need to enhance the capacity of teachers as generators of professional knowledge, in contrast to enhancing their capacity to apply someone else's knowledge, as with the findings of specialist researchers. A similar point is made by Schon (1983) in *The Reflective Practitioner*, as he examines the hierarchical model of professional development, in which research is institutionally separate from practice and connected to it by carefully defined relationships of exchange:

Researchers are supposed to provide the basic and applied science from which to derive techniques for diagnosing and solving the problems of practice. Practitioners are supposed to furnish researchers with problems for study and with tests of the utility of research results. The researcher's role is distinct from, and usually considered superior to, the role of the practitioner.

This view is part of the model of technical rationality, which Schon sees as the dominant epistemology of practice. According to the model of technical rationality, professional activity consists in 'instrumental problem solving made rigorous by the application of scientific theory and technique' (Schon, 1983). Technical rationality depends on agreement about ends. When ends are fixed and clear, then the decision to act can present itself, with reasonable justification, as an instrumental problem. The model breaks down when the ends are not clear and when the scientific theory fails to provide adequate or meaningful solutions. Further, the model does not of itself lead to increased understanding. We are thus trapped by our 'competence' and this leads to conflict. It is necessary to search laterally for a different approach in order to develop.

In school our attitude towards learning and teaching problems is often very restricted by this model. Learning theories might provide useful underlying concepts, such as positive reinforcement, recency, frequency, inhibition and so forth, but they do not offer us 'theory in action' and they seem not to help us in our deeper understanding of our practice and the way children learn. The model of technical rationality gives a view of the 'good' teacher as being a competent technician who can apply rules and knowledge skilfully. If either the rules are inadequate or inappropriate or the teacher is unwilling to apply them, we are unable to cope with the ensuing disorder.

There is a long-standing view that classroom problems reflect incompetence and lack of 'instrumental' skill. We do not have a tradition of sharing our difficulties, except perhaps in our early days of teaching, when we may seek help, particularly on matters of discipline, from more experienced colleagues. Teaching is a very insular business and behind the closed door of the classroom, expediency reigns. Hierarchical organisation tends to maintain teacher isolation and protects professional practice from critical analysis. Our reflections on our practice tend to remain a private affair and therefore we do not learn, collaboratively, how to make judgements about the quality of our teaching. We are not used to establishing, publicly, the criteria for making such judgements, yet every teacher has a way, within his own classroom, of assessing quality of learning. Our skilful performance depends on many recognitions, insights, understandings and judgements which constitute our educational intuition. We have, as Schon (1983) describes it, 'knowledge in action' and it is our reflection upon that 'knowing in action' which is central to the 'art' by which we deal with situations of uncertainty, instability, uniqueness, and value conflict. We improve our art through reflection and enquiry and this process is research, if it is systematic. Sadly, it may be that Schon has accurately described teacher outlook when he says 'many practitioners, locked onto a view of themselves as technical experts, find nothing in the world of practice to occasion reflection'. This is a view which we must repudiate with evidence of reflection-in-action.

When we recognise problems in pupil learning or wish to explore new ways of teaching and are unsure about the way to proceed, we may not have channels of communication which encourage open discussion of problems and of ways of solving them. Elliott & Adelman (1973b) recognised through their work on the Ford teaching project that many teachers find it difficult to discuss their problems with their colleagues, and the whole idea of self-evaluation is seen as threatening. If we do have the confidence to admit teaching concerns to others we can usually find a range of institutional excuses as to why we cannot properly tackle them in a systematic and enquiring way. Further, we might well hold back from making our attempts to solve problems or explore teaching issues a public matter in case they might fail. If we do start to think about our problems in a positive way, we realise the complexity of many classroom and learning issues and this makes us even less likely to start making claims to 'know' about our teaching. We need to be encouraged to establish enquiry networks and begin to turn the tide of educational research so that the benefits flow towards our children, through our own professional development.

In my view, the worst form of resistance to research is due to teacher competence — competent teachers feel that research is not necessary. A capable teacher, skilled in classroom management, able to teach the received syllabi effectively, does not perceive any need for research. Any suggestion that research could be helpful in developing understanding or improving practice is inferred as a threat or challenge to professional competence. This stems from the view of the teacher as a competent technician — already mentioned — adept at solving problems, adaptive in skill but chiefly instrumental and pragmatic in outlook. The pragmatic view is self-perpetuating; the more skilled we become at solving problems in an instrumental way, the less likely we are to accept criticism of our pragmatic judgements. These judgements, no matter how skilful, restrict the possibilities for growth and enrichment within the classroom (I refer to the sort of possibilities which grow out of reflection and critical discourse). However, the question is not whether our employers should decide between a teaching force of competent technicians or thoughtful and reflective educators, but how a marriage of the two roles can be achieved. Research demonstrates one possible way.

Hutchinson & Whitehouse (1986) believe that asking teachers to engage in research constitutes a fundamental challenge to existing notions of competence, since it means negating the meaning teachers have given to professional competence. In research the teacher is asked to accept the contradiction rather than the correspondence between thought and reality, and this is potentially threatening. As Patten (1986) has said, we need a non-threatening way of saying that improvement and change are desirable and necessary without implying an absolute abyss of professional competence and knowledge. Teachers who have learned the value of reflective self-criticism, without loss of status or competence, need to speak out in favour of research as a basis for teaching. Stenhouse (1979) holds that the documentation of the problems encountered by good teachers is a better basis for improving one's own practice than the documentation of best practice, and that 'We shall only teach better if we learn intelligently from the experience of shortfall, both in our grasp of the knowledge we offer and our knowledge of how to offer it. That is the case for research as a basis for teaching' (Stenhouse, 1979). Rudduck & Hopkins (1985) have expressed their challenge to current notions of competence:

> Research underlines the provisionality of knowledge. Teaching, at every level, is vulnerable if it does not acknowledge that error is a realistic intellectual achievement and failure a realistic practical achievement, for a critical appreciation of error and failure is a necessary foundation for improvement. Research, which disciplines curiosity and calls certainty into question, is a proper basis for teaching.

Unfortunately, we lack the time and encouragement to plan and pursue research projects or enquiries. Open acknowledgement of the importance of developing and improving the quality of teaching through our own participation in research is necessary. It will require considerable generosity, both financially and politically, on the part of our employers if they are to give their support to the 'teacher-researcher' movement. There would be some gain for employers, in that the skills involved in teacher research, particularly those of reflection, self-evaluation and critical analysis, are crucial to the successful introduction of the current plans for appraisal. 'Evaluation and appraisal demand skill and sensitivity. Training is necessary for all those involved, particularly in the process of evaluation itself including classroom observation and interviewing' (DES, 1985). We await details of the progress of the six local education authority (LEA) pilot projects, with particular interest in the Somerset proposal, which places the desire of teachers to improve their performance in order to benefit their pupils at the centre of its appraisal scheme.

The setting for my own research was an 11–18 urban comprehensive school. The investigation constitutes an example of professional development through curriculum development, using the paradigm of emancipatory action research to develop and improve the quality of personal and social education for the pupils. Once embarked upon my study, I realised quickly that research offers 'a way of structuring a familiar situation that allows the teacher to explore it in depth, gain new insights, set new goals and achieve new levels of competence and confidence' (Rudduck, 1985). As I familiarised myself with the action research paradigm I saw how I could tackle problems that were grounded in practice, using a research approach which offered opportunities for systematic enquiry and reflection, whilst remaining in tune with practice. This form of research is couched in straightforward language, the underlying concepts are simple and applicable to any situation and the method helps the researcher to see ordinary situations with new eyes, enabling understanding to develop in a liberated way. Ruddock (1985) likens this 'new' perspective of the teacher-turned-researcher to art, in that 'art teaches the sensitivity of being attentive to significances that would normally remain uncelebrated'. A similar view is also held by Nixon (1981): 'Action research serves primarily to sharpen perceptions, stimulate discussion and encourage questioning.' The comment by John Barnes (1960), 'a research understanding of the classroom group promotes better teaching', summarises most succinctly the value of research in improving practice. Barnes describes the two-way relationship between research and teaching: 'The process of descriptive research on the nature of the classroom group helps to develop a broad conception of what research really is and how it can serve the teacher.'

Action research is a form of enquiry which 'enables teachers to critically reflect on their classroom experience and write personal accounts of this experience' (Whitehead, 1983b). The teacher is a participant in the research and is central to the process. This is very different from other forms of research, such as the 'research–development–diffusion' model of educational progress which diminishes the role of the teacher. Skilbeck (1984) has acknowledged the vital part that teachers play in curriculum development: 'teacher awareness, understanding and skill play a central part in effecting an innovation'. Here curriculum development or innovation may be taken in its broadest sense to cover any improvement in the learning process, provided that it is part of a rationally ordered process. Consequently, research and development which does not involve the teacher at the centre of the development process is likely to have little effect in changing teaching behaviour and attitudes. Action research begins with the teacher's perceptions of what is happening in her or his classroom and essentially involves 'a process of self-reflective enquiry undertaken by participants in social or educational situations in order to improve the rationality and justification of their own educational practice, their understanding of these practices and the situations in which these practices are carried out' (Kemmis & Henry, 1984).

The case for action research has been stated by Nixon (1981) who believes that the teacher who engages in action research is not a special kind of teacher, but simply one who wishes to increase his or her professional expertise. By investigating and reflecting upon their own practice, teachers may increase their understanding of the classroom. The understanding derived may be acted upon, for it informs the teacher's judgement about such things as how children learn, what the critical moments in the learning process are, and how and when the teacher should intervene so as to facilitate this process. In addition, action research may also bring about a modification or elaboration of theories of teaching and learning. Research may be seen as an ongoing professional duty. It makes explicit the teaching acts; it informs them and enables the practitioner to understand the context in which they are embedded.

I found action research stimulating because it challenged me to look at my own practices and test ideas and assumptions about them. It satisfies curiosity in that it makes us think about meanings and begin the process of theorising about our practice, thereby leading us to a better understanding of practice. Action research fosters enthusiasm and can even 'generate excitement' (Rudduck, 1985), particularly when the potential for posing more powerful questions is realised. These positive feelings and attitudes are directed towards the actual practice of teaching. Any learning process which engenders enthusiasm within the teaching act has immediate worth for both pupil and teacher and has potential implications for improving the quality of education. Action research is not like attending an in-service course and feeling excited and motivated by the course, and then getting back to school and finding that there is a large gap between reality and the new intentions. Bridging this gap always requires considerable effort and often the effects of in-service training can evaporate away, leaving little to show for the investment.

I have found action research helpful in developing ways of assessing and evaluating the effectiveness of my teaching. The initial challenge is either to think about aspects of practice which need improving, or consider values which are being negated, or begin an attempt to understand practice better. Accepting this challenge in a learning way leads to a fundamental change in attitude for the teacher involved. To talk positively of changes desired, or problems encountered or negation of values leads directly into an enquiry mode. Reflection becomes a dominant activity and it becomes legitimate to talk about problems, question meanings or search for understanding. A major attitude-hurdle is overcome and this leads to a sense of liberation and growth. Learning can now be seen clearly and truly as a developmental process and the dialectical approach is the appropriate way forward. Action research satisfies the teachers' view given by Mitchell (1985) that 'at every level research should be helping us to question our assumptions and to move confidently to embrace alternative ways of working'.

Balanced against a somewhat euphoric transformation of attitude to the development of my teaching was a certain feeling of being limited by the form of the paradigm. I see now that this was because my understanding of action research had not yet grown. At the start of my study I was aware that I was trying to understand and develop several very complex issues relating to my field. When I first encountered the action research model I felt its simplicity of form to be incongruous with the complex nature of my study. I was reluctant to break the wholeness of what I was doing into logically distinct components, yet I felt the model called for the identification of a series of small, almost trivial problems. I could not define simple enough starting points, partly because I was involved in the very complex issues of personal and social education and partly because I interpreted the model in too concrete a form. It was only gradually that I came to learn that action research is as relevant to philosophical considerations as it is to the more practical matters of the teaching situation. I can see that travel from the concrete level to that of meanings is an easier journey compared with a path that starts with meanings. However, the delight of action research is the discovery that those meanings lie embedded in the practice, and action research offers ways of revealing them through a systematic form of enquiry which can generate the 'theory in practice'.

Although initially I felt constrained by the model, I was able to pursue my study by deciding not to see the model as a strait-jacket. Retrospectively, I can see that, in a sense, my reluctance to split my work into categories or discrete elements, according to the rationale of the disciplines approach, was in keeping with the spirit of action research. The model has two dimensions — its usefulness in organising activity, which has the potential either to constrain or create opportunities for development, and the more creative aspects which open up possibilities for growth. I think that constraint may be avoided by focusing on the qualitative aspects of the action research paradigm, which transcend the content or method. The latter has value as the basic *modus operandi*, giving form and direction to the research. The qualitative aspects — enquiring, reflective, understanding, creative, generative — give action research its special value to the practice being studied.

Stenhouse (1981b) says of the relationship between the curriculu
the research process: 'Action research relates to the curriculum in such a way
that the curriculum constitutes a definition and specification of the
experimental procedure.' Action research begins with a concept of what we are
trying to do, in other words, with a concept which is relevant and meaningful
to the living case. The concept will have grown out of perceived reality and a
desire to effect some sort of change or development or understanding.
Clarification of aims and objectives will contribute to improved
understanding of practice and, I believe, better practice. The initial concept
has a momentum, or at least a potential for movement, which is very different
from traditional forms of empirical research which do not seek to bring about
development directly through the research process. This gives action research
value or point for the practising teacher, since it offers three possibilities — of
improved practice, of improved understanding of practice and of
improvement in the situation in which the practice takes place. Though
aspects of the research work may be descriptive, this dynamic underlies the
approach and can be used to draw out principles of practice.

The practical aspects of action research are easy for teachers to
understand. Action research begins with teachers 'committed to learning
about and understanding the problems and effects of their own strategic
action and the improvement of this strategic action in practice' (Carr &
Kemmis, 1986). Strategies of planned action are implemented and then
systematically submitted to observation and reflection. This leads to change
or development. Cycles can begin in whatever way is appropriate to the
teacher and can relate to any aspect or concern relevant to the teacher's work.
The methods of enquiry or techniques for monitoring in action research are
open to choice. Most of those given by Kemmis & McTaggart (1981) in their
Action Research Planner are the sort of methods familiar to most teachers —
anecdotal records, field notes, diaries, logs, interviews, descriptions of
behaviour, practical documents, collections of materials, audio and video tape
recordings, photographs and slides, students' work and tests. Other methods,
suggested by various authors, might require some help initially but are well
within the grasp of all teachers; for example, sociometric methods, interaction
schedules, checklists and 'triangulation'. The important point is that the
methods must be used systematically and rigorously and the evidence
generated is subjected to reflection and the critical scrutiny of others. The
nature of the evidence presented in support of claims to know one's practice is
open and can take a variety of forms. The teacher needs to be aware that the
evidence can be in many forms and thus she should be alert to recognising
valuable evidence, since it is possible to omit recording or documenting vital
evidence.

The action research process is dependent on dialectic, as in the art of asking questions, and 'will prove itself only because the person who knows how to ask questions is able to persist in asking questions' (Gadamer, 1975). Cycles of action research lead to further enquiry if the researcher is able to sustain the dialectic or is not prevented by external constraints. The teacher-researcher has to be prepared for this developmental implication and for change. The teacher asking questions conducts a real conversation about his practice and this, says Whitehead, leads to a transformation in which we do not remain as we were.

Action research has the potential to close the gap between the way I would like to see the world, with my set of values, aims and ideals, and the world of my practice, my classroom and the educational setting of that classroom. Through the dialectic I can move nearer to living out my values and reducing the tension between the two, which casts me in the role of a 'living contradiction' (Whitehead, 1986). The logic of this aspect of the model is reasonable but it makes assumptions with which I have difficulty. I reason thus:

> I act from conviction that my values and aims are in the best interests of the education of my pupils. Therefore, I feel justified in pursuing research which seeks to negate the negation of my values in practice. But, I cannot suppose that my values have universal truth or validity.

Collingwood (1978) has examined the idea of truth and distinguishes between 'right' and 'true'. He defines the 'right' answer to a question as the answer which enables us to pursue the process of questioning and answering. He uses 'truth' to refer to the whole structure or complex of questions and answers, in which each question and answer in a given complex has to be relevant to the whole and to the place occupied in the whole. Adapting Collingwood's differentiation, I have used 'right' for correctness of the dialectic, 'true' for the relationship it holds to my concept of education, and 'value' for the worth of my concept of education. Translating this into practical terms, as an educator I believe there must be three aspects to the justification of my practice:

(1) justification of the process of teaching and of research (*the 'rightness' of the dialectic*)

(2) justification of the relevance of the process to my concept of education (*the degree to which this process is 'true' to my concept of education*)

(3) justification of the value of my concept of education (*the 'value' of my concept of education with respect to a wide range of issues relevant to education*).

My research has focused on the justification for the process of teaching and learning, and references to the ideology which guides my practice have been implicit. Although questions about the value or worth of my concept of education have been posed as an integral part of my practice — in the in-service work of curriculum development and the improvement of my own teaching — the issue has not been tackled from a philosophical perspective, and it may be that this will be perceived as a weakness in the action research enquiry into ways of developing and improving personal and social education. I cannot find, from my reading and discussion, whether the action research paradigm requires the second and third stages of justification which I have outlined, and I feel this is an aspect which needs clarification for teachers.

There are other disadvantages to the action research model. Some of these centre on the aspect of action research that implies change, and change has the potential to be very threatening. Change within an individual classroom may be fairly acceptable to others provided it does not impinge upon them. Change involving other teachers is accepted by other teachers if they feel party to the decisions surrounding the change. Imposed change can be disastrous. Change involving a group of teachers is acceptable to 'authority' provided it complies with given policy. Change which challenges existing structures or invites others to justify their practice, in institutions which are not conversant with research-based development, is not welcome. Hutchinson & Whitehouse (1986) hold that 'by offering to challenge the values embedded in the social reality in order to improve it action research is perceived as a threat not only to the hierarchy but also to notions of competence that assistant teachers have'.

Action research implies change growing outwards from individual classrooms in ever increasing circles which involve the whole school, the governing body and the local education authority. If change moves upwards, i.e. in the opposite direction to normal in the hierarchy of change, then constraining forces are likely to emerge, in an attempt to dampen the perceived threat. This presents a conflict for the teacher-researcher. At what point does one stop the cycles of enquiry? The model implies that, in the pursuit of enquiry and the development of professionalism, the teacher-researcher will move on from the setting of his classroom to the wider educational setting. Intellectual honour and professional integrity would motivate the teacher to continue study for the educational benefit of his pupils. Expediency may caution the teacher to avoid challenges which may have career repercussions.

In short, action research can have very powerful political implications and this potential power strengthens the value of the paradigm. It does, however, make it less likely that action research will be favoured by institutions wishing to protect their own forms of professional management and their power structures. An individual pursuing his own study within established institutional parameters is relatively harmless and also has relatively little chance of making any impact; I would think that communities of enquirers would receive more attention and have a greater chance of achieving recognition for the potential of action research for professional development and for improving the quality of education. However, Hutchinson and Whitehouse report that this is not necessarily the case. They claim that action research and educational institutions have dichotomous polar tendencies such that there is a dialectical tension between them. This leads to a struggle between two 'political' realities in which action research 'loses' and the power of collaborative groups is rendered neutral.

The potential of action research is considerable and the political will to develop this potential needs to be clarified. Implicit in the model of action research is the development of communities of enquirers. There is much educational progress to be made through groups of teachers working together, sharing their problems, their experience and their understanding of practice in a constructive and developmental way. Collaboration, in enquiry and critical reflection, through the creative and emancipatory model of action research, offers considerable possibilities for improving the quality of education for our pupils.

3   A guide to action research

DAVID FORWARD

Action research has been described as the 'alternative paradigm' (Elliott, 1981) whose methods 'offer a promise of transforming the whole field of educational research' (Nisbett, 1980). It has been defined as '. . . a science which seeks to inform action through articulated experience of prior action'. (Brown, Henry & McTaggart, 1982).

Its appropriateness to studies of curriculum innovation and development has been supported by Nisbett (1980) who saw research and innovation being fused together in interventionist-type studies called action research, in which '. . . research monitors change, research is a guide to action and the results of action are a guide to research'.

Kemmis & Henry (1984) also saw action research as suitable for curriculum development:

> Action research is a form of self-reflective enquiry undertaken by participants in social (including educational) situations in order to improve the rationality and justice of (a) their own social or educational practices, (b) their understanding of these practices, and (c) the situations in which these practices are carried out. It is most rationally empowering when undertaken by participants collaboratively, though it is often undertaken by individuals, and sometimes in co-operation with 'outsiders'. In education, action research has been employed on school-based curriculum development, professional development, school improvement programs, and systems planning and policy development.

Such literature indicates that this type of research holds considerable potential for a teacher-researcher wanting simultaneously to implement and evaluate a curriculum innovation. Furthermore, action research draws on the widest possible range of methods as it encompasses techniques from all the traditional methodological paradigms.

The Origins and Development of Action Research

'Action research' was a term originated by Kurt Lewin, referring to research involving experimental interventions in institutions and communities (Lewin, 1946). The Lewinian version of action research differed from its modern counterparts by being externally initiated to assist a client system, normative in orientation and prescriptive in practice (Hopkins, 1984). However, Lewin's basic research cycle of planning, executing and reconnaissance or fact-finding to allow evaluation and further planning (Lewin, 1948) has become an integral part of many subsequent action research projects by forming the basis for the action research cycle.

The credibility of action research and teacher-based research was greatly enhanced by the Humanities Curriculum Project led by Lawrence Stenhouse which encouraged a critically reflective attitude to teaching on the part of teachers. Stenhouse saw the extended professional teacher as one who adopted the action research model to achieve '. . . a capacity for autonomous professional development through systematic self-study, through the work of other teachers and through the testing of ideas by classroom research procedures' (Stenhouse, 1975). This view strongly influenced the Ford Teaching Project, an action research enquiry into new methods of teaching in primary schools which, largely due to the work of Clem Adelman and John Elliott, led to the formation of CARN (Classroom Action Research Network) in Cambridge in 1976. CARN produces regular bulletins containing reports of a variety of action research projects. Other influential action research groups include Stephen Kemmis and his colleagues at Deakin University in Australia, and SWARN (South-West Action Research Network) led by Jack Whitehead at Bath University.

With such diverse groups the emphasis given to various characteristics of action research will inevitably vary, although the main characteristics are shared. The most important of these for my work have been:

Action research seeks improvement by intervention;

Action research is responsive;

Action research is a disciplined enquiry;

Action research is participatory;

Action research requires validation.

(See Lomax, 1986a)

The Characteristics of Action Research

Action research seeks improvement by intervention

According to its proponents action research '. . . uses strategic action as a probe for improvement and understanding' (Brown *et al.*, 1982). This helps to '. . . further the solution of practical educational problems' (Brock-Utne, 1980). Action researchers do not claim terminal solutions to problems but do claim to improve practice through the educational development of the participants and the theories that conceptualise such development. Kemmis & McTaggart (1981) have stated: •

> You do not have to begin with a 'problem'. All you need is a general idea that something might be improved. Your general idea may stem from a promising new idea or the recognition that existing practice falls short of aspiration. In either case you must centre attention on:

— What is happening now?

— In what sense is this problematic?

— What can I do about it?

The answer to the third question determines the nature of the intervention and the initial course of the action and research. Henry (1986) suggests that this is likely to lead to reconceptualisation of theory, which in turn informs curriculum decision making and effects curriculum change.

Action research is responsive

Action research adopts an interactive approach to the improvement of educational practice. This differs from the purely objective approach of the quantitative paradigm and from the more passive forms of qualitative research.

Action research is responsive because it is a method of solving an educational problem such as 'How do I improve this process of education here?' (Whitehead, 1984). It is also responsive because it not only monitors and records but reacts to feedback from the participants in each of its research and intervention sequences. This is reflected in the spiral models of action research such as the one suggested by Kemmis & McTaggart (1981) where each cycle of the spiral involves a deliberate sequence of events informed by the response of the participants to the previous action.

Action research is a disciplined enquiry

Action research is based on systematic procedures sharing the scientific character of the Popperian schema which explains how scientists go about their work of generating knowledge (Whitehead, 1984). The schema:

I experience problems

I imagine solutions

I act in the direction of the imagined solution

I evaluate the outcome of my action

I modify my problems, ideas, action in the light of my evaluation

indicates the main phases of a research process and is intended to assist in the solution of research problems (Popper, 1972). In educational research an action cycle can be used similarly to assist the researcher working with the research problem or the practitioner seeking to improve practice. It is a means of identifying crucial stages in the development of theory about practice and of increasing the responsiveness, sensitivity and overall success of the action research project. However, it is not 'the scientific method' applied to education. Kemmis & Henry (1984) state of action research:

> Its view is distinct from the methods of the historical sciences because action research is concerned with changing situations, not just interpreting them. Action research is a systematically-evolving, lived process of changing both the researcher and the situations in which he or she acts; neither the natural sciences nor the historical sciences have this double aim (the living dialectic of researcher and researched).

The practitioners of action research generally operate within the qualitative/ interpretive paradigm although some workers support the use of statistical methods if they are used appropriately (eg. Brock-Utne, 1980). In most action research, positivistic notions of rationality, objectivity and truth are rejected (Lomax, 1986c), being replaced by an open view about what counts as evidence (Kemmis & Henry, 1984). This demands rigour and is not an excuse for a sloppy or poorly conceived methodology (Chambers, 1983). The use of the action research cycle contributes to this rigour as does the practice of 'critical self-reflection' (Brown *et al.*, 1982) which is a form of self-study and self-analysis essential to action enquiry. Kemmis & Henry (1984) indicate that this entails the keeping of detailed personal records:

> which describe what is happening as accurately as possible (given the particular questions being investigated and the real-life circumstances of collecting the data) but also collecting and analysing our own judgements, reactions and impressions about what is going on.

and a personal diary,

> in which we record our progress and our reflections about two parallel sets of learning: our learning about the practice we are studying (how our practices are developing) and our learnings about the process (the practice) of studying them (how our action research project is going).

Such techniques are regarded as an important part of action research and help to confirm that it is not pseudo-research but a disciplined form of enquiry with a clear methodology rigorously applied. It is *the* paradigm for much pedagogic research.

Action research is participatory

Action research involves some type of social or educational intervention and therefore it is only good sense that the practitioners involved should participate. The practitioners should have a clear understanding and first-hand experience of the research situation, and therefore be able to produce the action response which triggers the next phase of the research cycle. Action research does not treat people as statistics or objects but regards them as autonomous and responsible participants in the process under investigation. This can lead to a growth of the collaborating or participating group as the research proceeds (Kemmis & Henry, 1984). However, in reporting on a number of small-scale action research projects, Elliott (1979) discovered that teachers researched as isolated individuals in six out of the 12 schools involved, indicating a collapse of the aspiration of broad collaborative research. Clearly the participative and collaborative intentions of action research are not always achieved. One of Elliott's research groups commented: 'Undercurrents among the staff may make it impossible for any individual or group within a school to initiate or sustain either (a) collaborative action-research among staff, or (b) staff co-operation with the teacher-researchers in the school.' Subsequently, Holly (1984) has written: 'Given the opportunity of putting into action their alternative conceptions of the schooling process, action researchers often find that their institutions display many and varied ingenious devices to normalize their activities'. But despite the problems experienced by some practitioners regarding collaboration it remains an important principle in action research (Chambers, 1983).

Action research requires validation

Validation is the process of ratifying or confirming the authenticity and reliability of research findings. Like any other research method action research requires validation to demonstrate the truth of the research and to enhance its credibility. This is particularly so of action research because of the need to convince outsiders of its effectiveness. Questions of validation addressed to action research are often grounded wrongly in the view that it consists of the application of positivistic scientific theory and technique to a problem of educational practice (Whitehead, 1984). The complexities of the social milieu in which most research projects are located denies the proper use of control experiments or the replication of situations for scientific validation, and so alternative methods for assessing validity have evolved.

Validation is not guaranteed by rigour, although generally the more detailed the research methodology the more convincing the outcomes are likely to be, especially if multiple methods are employed. The use of a range of techniques such as detailed descriptions of situations, events, people and interactions, together with the use of direct quotations, interviews and questionnaires is convincing, particularly when quantitative and qualitative data are juxtaposed. Action research, it is claimed, is more than a private encounter between practitioner and practice (Foster, 1984) although self-validation is central to the validation process (Whitehead, 1985a). Whitehead has indicated that until individual researchers are themselves convinced of the relevance and true worth of what they know they should not make their claims public. Peer-practitioner validation, where action researchers present their self-validated claims for debate by co-practitioners, is suggested as the next stage (Whitehead, 1985a). This links validation to the participative and collaborative aims of action research, and contrasts with other research which for validation looks towards academic research communities who are mainly interested in education as a field for applying their own scientific disciplines (Bassey, 1980).

A technique particularly useful to action researchers for assessing reliability and aiding validation is triangulation. This was a method developed by Elliott and Adelman during their work on the Ford Teaching Project. It involves comparing the views of one person or group in a research situation with those of others in the same situation. Elliott & Adelman (1976) describe triangulation as:

> gathering accounts of a teaching situation from three quite different points of view; namely, those of the teacher, his pupils, and a participant observer. Who in the 'triangle' gathers the accounts, how they are elicited, and who compares them, depends largely on the context. The process of gathering accounts from three distinct standpoints has an epistemological position with respect to access to relevant data about a teaching situation. The teacher is in the best position to gain access by introspection to his own intentions and aims in the situation. The students are in the best position to explain how the teacher's actions influence the way they respond in the situation. The participant observer is in the best position to collect data about the observable features of the interaction between teachers and pupils. By comparing his own account with accounts from the other two standpoints a person at one point of the triangle has an opportunity to test and perhaps revise it on the basis of more sufficient data.

Clearly such an approach is directed towards classroom research but it can easily be extended to apply to a wider area of educational research. Denzin (1978) has identified four main triangulation types: data triangulation using a variety of data sources; investigator triangulation using different researchers or evaluators; theory triangulation using different perspectives to interpret data; and methodological triangulation using multiple methods to study a single event or programme.

Using action research

Action research with its emphasis on improvement of practice by intervention was adopted as the paradigm for my research at Albury School, where I aimed to bring about an improvement in pastoral provision for pupils (Forward, 1988).

My initial answer to the question 'What is happening now?' was that an inefficient process of pastoral care was operative, and which had all the hallmarks of the 'crisis model'. It was 'problematic' because the pastoral process seemed inadequate both in terms of staff efficiency due to the dominance of the 'tutor subordinate' model (Marland, 1974) and in terms of pupil effectiveness. My response to this insight based on a fusion between my own ideas and the available literature was that the quality and quantity of pastoral care needed to be improved by developing a 'preventative model' which utilised a pastoral curriculum (Forward, 1986). I saw the responsiveness of action research coupled to my collaborative intentions as an important feature of this research mode likely to influence both the direction and the outcome of my work. This was facilitated by the adoption of an action cycle which included a reflection stage as one of its components.

One of the advantages of using a research cycle as a discipline was that I could research my action of developing and implementing a pastoral curriculum by using both quantitative and qualitative techniques. In particular I developed a research diary (Burgess, 1981) which contained records of conversations, actions taken and their subsequent effects, my own feelings and thought processes on particular issues as well as ideas and reminders for future consideration. This diary was developed from numerous jottings on pieces of paper (less noticeable) and formed the basis for the personal weekly review and planning sessions which I now consider to have been essential to the success of my research. All notes for my research diary were meticulously referenced by teacher number, circumstances, time and date.

My reading of Elliott's action research group reports (Elliott, 1979) warned that a public declaration of my research intentions would possibly lead to staff division and result in data collection problems. Teacher-researchers can be viewed with suspicion and be seen as threatening by their colleagues (Woods, 1977) and they can be denied access to data (Burgess, 1980). In order to ensure the viability of my research I adopted a bipartite solution to this problem by distinguishing methodologically between two roles which I performed simultaneously. In my role as curriculum developer I worked overtly and collaboratively with my colleagues whilst in my role as teacher-researcher I worked covertly on my own. Although it is a reversal of his example, Burgess would probably regard my approach as 'semi-covert research' as I discussed my role with the headmaster and senior deputy head but not my colleagues or pupils. This adoption of a semi-covert research stance was to prevent any deliberate institutional normalisation of my research activities (Holly, 1984) and to allow me to research unimpeded within Albury School.

Of particular relevance to my research programme was the triangulation of data sources to check the consistency of information received at different times and using different means. Patton (1980) suggested that this should involve:

a. Comparing observational data with interview data;

b. Comparing what people say in public with what they say in private;

c. Checking the consistency of what people in a situation say about the situation over time;

d. Comparing the perspectives of people from different points of view.

Following the views of Best *et al.* (1979, 1983) I decided to opt for the multiple-method approach and to triangulate as much data as I could to check the reliability of my findings. This allowed discrepancies between data sources to be investigated and, linked to my action methodology, they greatly enhanced the accuracy and validity of my research.

I considered two models of action research when deciding which methodology would be most appropriate. The first model was the action spiral of Kemmis & McTaggart (1981) and the second the action research model of Elliott (1981). Kemmis & McTaggart suggested an action cycle of planning, acting, observing and reflecting. This was linked to further cycles of action research to form a spiral. Preceding the action spiral was what Kemmis termed a 'reconnaissance' phase which involved preparation for action by previous analysis and fact-finding (Ebbutt, 1983). The relative simplicity of Kemmis's helical model was in contrast with Elliott's more complex model which attempted to demonstrate more of the 'messiness' of the action research process. Elliott's model was also multi-cyclic but based upon a more complicated sequence including planning, action, monitoring and reconnaissance.

Although both models revealed many similarities I adopted Kemmis's action spiral as my overall research strategy. This model was chosen because:

1. It was most similar to a recurring cyclical pattern of observation, analysis and change which I had already identified in planning my research.

2. It seemed simpler to use. I found that I could only construct an accurate Elliott-type model in retrospect, which although useful for review and reflection was not useful for anticipation or prediction.

3. It allowed for my work to commence at the reconnaissance stage with observation and reflection rather than with any identifiable initial idea. Elliott's model seemed to imply that identifying the initial idea was the starting point.

Developing a Research Strategy

My overall research and development programme divided into two main phases. Initially, my pre-action research or 'reconnaissance' phase (Kemmis & McTaggart, 1981) involved a review of the pastoral literature and a consideration of the possibilities of developing an effective pastoral curriculum in Albury School. This took two years. Subsequently my 'action research' phase involved collaboration with the staff at Albury School to develop and implement a pastoral curriculum. This involved working parties, staff conferences and numerous other meetings over a four-year period (Forward, 1988).

During the six years of the project my role underwent considerable change. As the new pastoral curriculum was implemented, feedback from the staff indicated that my aim to devolve responsibility for the pastoral programme component to the pastoral year teams was achieved. Use of the planning, acting, observing and reflecting components of the action research cycle led me to engage form teachers and heads of year in their own evaluation and improvement programme. Not only did this provide the means of further enhancing pastoral programme provision, but also it provided informed opinion to effect further change.

As the new programmes were used my role as curriculum developer underwent change. From being the initiator of a major pastoral overhaul I became more an equal participant as each of the year teams focused on their own pastoral programme. In addition to broadening ownership of the pastoral curriculum this had the added advantage of preventing major disturbance when I was appointed to a different role as deputy head in the same school.

My research role also underwent change during the project as I experienced a conflict between my need to acquire research data and my aim to devolve ownership of the pastoral programme to the year teams. Much of the data generated about pastoral programmes and their use was not formally available to me as the year teams increasingly took on a monitoring and evaluation role. Although some data were shown to me informally, this was generally selected by heads of year to highlight successes or problems and did not provide me with an effective overview. In anticipation of a reducing volume of data my use of the action research cycle led me to supplement my formative-type evaluation strategy with data of a more summative type. This was achieved by attitude surveys and data from interviews with staff conducted by an outside interviewer.

Coping with these role and research changes was facilitated by the flexibility and responsiveness of the action research approach which through the action research cycle informed my work and heightened my awareness of my influence on it. This resulted not only in the project being a whole-school pastoral reorganisation but also a personal learning process as the action cycle helped me to use findings from previous work to plan future development. In using the 'alternative paradigm' (Elliott, 1981) of action research I was able simultaneously to research and catalyse this collaborative curriculum development. The action research characteristics of responsiveness, improvement through intervention and disciplined enquiry contributed significantly to the effectiveness with which I was able to intervene in the process of pastoral care in Albury School, and to the improvement in pastoral philosophy and practice that resulted.

4   A question of dialectics

ANDY LARTER

Walker (1985) suggests that:

> It is a fundamental belief in science, and one which has been carried over to social science and educational research, that research is primarily reported to the scientific peer group. It is this 'invisible college' which scrutinizes research, and through a process of critical debate and a 'free market' mechanism of acknowledgement and reference, admits it to the status of received wisdom.

My enquiry has been carried out by using the insights of colleagues in an open manner: I *wanted* to discuss the things I found in my practice and I make no apology for doing so. Walker also says: 'The very form of the dialogue makes a point not made in other ways. It invites participation; in itself it rejects . . . an authoritative judgement; it demonstrates 'open-endedness', divergence of view, unresolved conflict and discrepancy in a manner that statements cannot.'

This leads me to the work of Gadamer. His 'logic of question and answer' is one aspect of dialectics which I find very helpful:

> The art of dialectic is not the art of being able to win every argument. On the contrary, it is possible that someone who is practising the art of dialectic, i.e. the art of questioning and seeking truth, comes off worse in the argument in the eyes of those listening to it. Dialectic, as the art of asking questions, proves itself only because the person who knows how to ask questions is able to persist in his questioning, which involves being able to preserve his orientation towards openness. The art of questioning is that of being able to go on asking questions, i.e. the art of thinking. It is called 'dialectic' for it is the art of conducting a real conversation . . . Dialectic consists not in trying to discover the weakness of what is said, but in bringing out its real strength. It is not the art of arguing that is able to make a strong case out of a weak one, but the art of thinking that is able to strengthen what is said by referring to the object. (Gadamer, 1975)

The importance of Gadamer's thinking on the subject of question and answer seems to me to lie in the idea of dialogue and, once again, immersion in or commitment to the case at hand.

Why is the logic of question and answer or dialectics so important? There are, I think, a couple of reasons. First of all, the implication is that through the process of formulating questions I, the practitioner, can really probe the meaning of events. As Kitwood (1976) says, 'To practitioners of education, tentative or incomplete answers to significant questions are of more value than excellently contrived answers to trivial or trumped up problems'. I could not agree more, and so the process of finding the right question is of great moment. And who is in a better position to ask such questions than the practitioner herself? Of course, it is always possible, in fact desirable, to discuss these questions along the lines suggested by Gadamer above. A further way in which this process is useful and important is in the realisation that there are always questions to be asked. Just as the action–reflection cycle is continuous, so is the process of question and answer: they mesh together. In looking at my practice, I realise that there are a lot of questions that need to be answered — not because it is a bad practice, but because it is social and therefore problematic, just as all social events are. Ilyenkov (1977) is helpful on this subject: 'Contradiction as the concrete unity of mutually exclusive opposites is the real nucleus of dialectics, its central category.' This is helpful in that I believe this is the way in which development takes place.

Can you show how this development takes place? An example from my own practice would be an incident when some fourth-year boys gave me a racist poem to read. This conflicted with my feelings about racism and I attempted to deal with the issue in the lesson. Quite clearly here was an occasion where one value I hold was in conflict with the values of the boys. I think that this is how most arguments come about. I attempted to argue with the boys about the poem and the dangerous attitudes I thought it opened up; this was my perception of the situation anyway. What happened was filmed because I had a video camera in the room at the time, and I had to live with the other issues raised for me by the film. Apart from the embarrassment I felt about the things I said and the way I said them, there are many contradictions apparent in the episode. For instance, there was the denial of my express desire to allow students opportunities to discuss ideas because I feel that this is an important way of learning. What happened in my discussion with the boys was that I closed down such opportunities in my desire to convince them that this was a racist poem, and that they were behaving in a way which I thought was prejudiced and not based on sound knowledge. In short, I attempted to browbeat them into my way of thinking! (the incident is examined in much more detail in Larter, 1987).

It is the tension between the objects to be understood (e.g. phenomena in the classroom like the incident of the racist poem) and the action of the individuals who try to understand and improve them (e.g. my attempts to act upon the thinking of the boys in the racist poem incident) that actually moves our understanding forward. At the same time, there are internal contradictions which affect change and improvement. In the case of the racist poem incident, there were, within the episode, the contradictions between my educational values and the actual lived practice. Here, I was able to see myself as a 'living contradiction', to use Ilyenkov's (1977) phrase. It was the shock of seeing myself performing in that way which led me to consider ways of changing my practice to attempt to improve the process of education.

I also claim that dialectical knowledge can absorb formal logic because it is valuable as a tool of analysis and knowledge. Thus, the use of video film of the racist poem episode is, at one level, a way of slowing the incident down until it was static and could be analysed. But the limitation of this activity is that it does not tell me anything about what I intended to do as a potential way of improving the situation I analysed. As a way of understanding the motion of human activity, formal logic is severely limited. As soon as I was dealing with my attempts to improve the process of education in my practice, dialectical logic was imposed upon me. Thus, in the unity of my practice there was negation of my educational values. I found it very difficult to live out my values because of the conflicting demand made by different items within the same value system, i.e. my value of discussion as profound pedagogical method with my value of human rights and human worth: I denied one at the expense of the other. This was compacted with my values about truth and integrity. In such a situation, there must be contradiction of me as an individual attempting to live out my own educational values. The picture is further complicated by the denial of my educational values by the other actors in the incident: the boys. They, by their act of giving me the racist poem, contradicted my educational values in the sense that the poem was racist and therefore flew in the face of my desire to promote racial awareness and understanding, and also instigated the whole process of investigation into the way I deal with students' ideas in the classroom. It was through these contradictions that improvement took place: improvement of understanding and of practice, which in turn led to further contradictions.

This relationship between critical reflection on past action and the continuing struggle to improve the process of education forms a liberating experience of professional life. Essentially, I think this is because I realise that the impetus for change lies with me, not forgetting the influence that students and colleagues will have, through discussion and a shared approach to the events under scrutiny. I am attracted to the words of Paulo Freire (1985) (but do wish he would change his sexist language):

> The starting point for . . . . an analysis [of conscientization] must be a critical comprehension of man as a being who exists *in* and *with* the world. Since the basic condition for conscientization is that its agent must be a subject (i.e. a conscious being), conscientization, like education, is specifically and exclusively a human process. It is as conscious beings that men are not only *in* the world but *with* the world, together with other men. Only men, as 'open' beings, are able to achieve the complex operation of simultaneously transforming the world by their action and grasping and expressing the world's reality in their creative language . . . . Conscientization is viable only because men's consciousness, although conditioned, can recognize that it is conditioned. This 'critical' dimension of consciousness accounts for the goals men assign to their transforming acts upon the world. Because they are able to have goals, men alone are capable of entertaining the result of their action even before initiating the proposed action. They are beings who project.

It is this critical consciousness which is both liberating and progressive. This is not to say that the dialectic is merely cause and effect. One of the implications of a dialectical approach to understanding is that events are rooted in history and the actions of people. Thus, to return to the racist poem incident racism and anti-racism exist outside my classroom for historical reasons and the clash of ideas in the episode came about because of these factors, as well as because of the reasons pertaining to the personalities of the actors. But it is the tension between all the forces affecting the classroom that causes the development of practice, reflection and understanding. The dialectic is about attempting to understand the parts and the whole.

But if we are to accept Gadamer's idea that we are not yet ready for the logic of question and answer, where does this leave our thinking? Are we ready for dialectics? Now, here I come across another of the problems of the dialectic: it is not easy to throw off the products of a life of education which is individualistic and intellectual , which dichotomises theory and practice, and celebrates intellectual work at the expense of manual or professional labour. I sometimes find it very difficult to accept the criticism offered by students or colleagues, and any notion that in discussion with those mentioned in my writing there has been no struggle of power, status or experience is wrong. I believe that this is another aspect of the dialectic at work in my professional life — I am granted the status of an 'expert' and demand to be treated as such, despite my values about equality and dialogue. Again, I see myself as a 'living contradiction'. I believe that I must live with the problems and continue to try to improve. Without such contradiction, I would not be able to improve the quality of my work. I struggle to live out my values, yet find myself falling short; I struggle to understand my actions, and begin to do so in discussion with others. These are living forms of theory (McNiff, 1988).

So where does this help in an understanding of educational knowledge? It is self-reflective transformation of practice. As an action researcher I am endeavouring to bring my practice under self-reflective control through my commitment to rationality, truth, truthfulness and rightness. The implications of this are that I am critical of the ideological and institutional conditions which deny my attempts to bring about such control. It is also an attempt to bring about a unity of theory and practice, in the sense that by reflecting on my practice, I am interested in, indeed committed to, a 'critical revival of practice' (Carr & Kemmis, 1986) that is, to praxis. In turn, this intentional activity can only be studied by me because only I have the access to the commitments and professional theory which inform my practice. I am reminded that I ground my epistemology in personal knowledge (Polanyi, 1958) and that I struggle to

> retrospectively reconstruct an interpretation of the action in context as a basis for future action. Knowledge achieved in this way informs and refines both specific planning in relation to the practice being considered (i.e. my own) and the practitioner's general practical theory of education. (Carr & Kemmis, 1986)

Because my epistemology is grounded in personal knowledge (Polanyi, 1958) and in the dialectic, I felt I had to write in the first person to reflect this. This also serves to represent the struggles I have gone through to understand my practice retrospectively and to improve it.

How does action research fit in with all this about dialectics? In my personal experience, action research is a dialectical process through which we can come to understand our own practice. It is not merely a descriptive account of what went on in those lessons I have examined; it is also analytical and shows the struggles I underwent and my attempts to improve my practice over a period of time. Action research is a planned though commonsense process of:

— perceiving problems in my practice, relating to some of my educational values not being realised;

— imagining solutions to these problems;

— planning courses of action and acting in the direction of such plans;

— observing and gathering data as the plan is acted upon;

— reflecting upon the action and the data;

— modifying problems in the light of findings;

— imagining solutions to problems

and so on through a continuous cycle of action and reflection. The dynamic tension between the acting and reflecting moments of the cycle is the tension of dialectics, between theory and practice.

How does all this lead us to generalise from the case studies in this work and its like? I see generalisation as a complex concept. There is Polanyi's idea:

> The skilful performer is seen to be setting standards to himself and judging himself by them; the connoisseur is seen valuing comprehensive entities in terms of a standard set by him for their excellence. The elements of such a context . . . all point beyond themselves and are endowed with meaning in this context; and on the other hand a comprehensive context itself like dance, mathematics, music, possesses intrinsic or existential meaning. (Polanyi, 1958)

Thus, I can transcend my own intrinsic subjectivity by struggling to fulfil my personal commitment to universal standards. Polanyi argues that it is this intellectual commitment which makes personal knowledge more than merely subjective. My commitment to my work of attempting to improve the process of learning through action and reflection gives it, in this way, a universality of intention: that is, I make statements with universal intent not because my commitment compels me to do so but because the existential meaning of that act demands that I do so. To use Polanyi's words. 'commitment is a "shirt of flame", blazing with passion and . . . consumed by devotion to a universal demand' (Polanyi, 1958).

Also in my understanding of generalisability there is my idea of 'use-value'. This is my belief that my work is generalisable in the sense that someone else has found merit in it. To produce my work, I have used the work of others because I felt that there was merit in it. In my turn, I offer my work for others to use if it has use-value for them. So it is not possible to produce work without other work. It is this tension between our work and the work of others that moves human understanding forward.

Another facet of my concept of generalisation is the form of presentation. It really did take me a long time to work out this particular form. I wanted to maintain the dialogic nature of the work and yet integrate into it the ideas of educational and other academics as well as the discussions that went on in the classroom. However, the form of the dialogue is not all. It offers me the facility of allowing my work to have an ongoing, unfinished feel, which is in keeping with the question I have frequently asked, 'How do I/we improve this process of education here?'. Answers to this question cannot be finite: for me this is a continuous process. As Rob Walker says: 'The very form of the dialogue makes a point not made in other ways. It invites participation; in itself it rejects . . . an authoritative judgement; it demonstrates "open-endedness", divergence of view, unresolved conflict and discrepancy in a manner which statements cannot' (Walker, 1985).

But there is more to it than this too. I reckon that a dialogic form also speaks to a different audience than the 'traditional research establishment', to use a phrase from Walker (1985). One of my desires is to close the gap between theory and practice; this seems to me to be a good thing to do. I have tried to write a thesis which speaks to the educational research establishment as well as to a wider professional audience. I think that in using the form of the dialogue I have gone some way towards bringing these two branches of activity together.

5 In conversation with myself: becoming an action researcher

BARRIE JONES

Adventures in the Wild Woods

> The Rat crept into the hollow, and there he found the Mole, exhausted and still trembling. 'Oh, Rat!' he cried, 'I've been so frightened, you can't think!'
>
> 'Oh, I quite understand', said the Rat soothingly. 'You shouldn't really have gone and done it, Mole. I did my best to keep you from it. We river bankers, we hardly ever come here by ourselves. If we have to come, we come in couples, at least; then we're generally all right. Besides, there are a hundred things one has to know, which we understand all about and you don't, as yet. I mean pass-words, and signs, and sayings which have power and effect, and plants you carry in your pocket, and verses you repeat, and dodges and tricks you practise; all simple enough when you know them, but they've got to be known if you're small, or you'll find yourself in trouble.' (Grahame, 1977.)

Kenneth Grahame's classic story seems an unlikely source from which to embark on a research dialogue, yet to me the extract is a wry commentary on my tentative excursions into the research world. Apart from the potentially productive call for collaborative research, albeit for the wrong reasons, Rat's cautioning draws attention to obstacles which have, until recently, dissuaded me from venturing beyond the immediate boundary of the classroom in any real way.

The paternalistic tenor of Rat's 'good advice' is also a reminder that 'father' is always right, the all-illumined one, with the implication that 'the learner' is denied the possibility of growing towards autonomy — unless he/ she learn the established rules. Rowe's (1971) discussion of this point, in a context different from the one addressed in this chapter, is very apt. Following Rowe, one could say that for too long, the research community has pretended that things are other than they are; have engaged in humbug. Rowe quotes Bibby (1966) on the meaning of humbug: 'a means of evading full honesty without actually lying'.

For Rowe, the only position is Yevtushenko's:

Telling lies to the young is wrong.
Proving to them that lies are true is wrong.
Telling them that God's in his heaven
and all's well with the world is wrong.
The young know what you mean. The young are people.
Tell them the difficulties can't be counted,
and let them see not only what will be
but see with clarity these present times.
Say obstacles exist they must encounter,
sorrow happens, hardship happens.
The hell with it. Who never knew
the price of happiness will not be happy.
Forgive no error you recognise,
it will repeat itself, increase,
and afterwards our pupils
will not forgive in us what we forgave.

An imaginary friend

My story is about a novice researcher's continuing journey on the path of enlightenment; an educative journey that hopefully will enable me to travel to a vantage point where I may view the 'wild woods' from a different, less threatening perspective. This chapter is intended to help me travel along that route. Introduced by Diamond (1988) to the idea of using biography as a tool for self-understanding, my interest in this approach was given momentum by a book written by Boud and Griffin (1987); in which they discuss the potential of standing away from the process of one's learning in order to tease out and crystallise the development therein. These inputs stimulated my thinking and led me, eventually, to the idea of concocting an 'imaginary friend', an interlocutor, who would become a springboard for my self-reflection.

Before I ask my 'friend' to help, I think it will be useful if I provide an overview of what is to follow. In a nutshell, my aims in this chapter are to:

— make sense of where I am as a researcher through looking at my biography;

— explain my current research interest and explore my approach to it.

The chapter is written as a dialogue between myself (B.) and my imaginary friend (F.)

A Reluctant Researcher

F.   Barrie, I have some difficulty in reconciling aspects of your professional persona. On the one hand you are a teacher whom I know to have an open mind, interested in and available to new ideas, yet you are also a teacher who has not engaged in research. You agree with Popper (1972), that nothing endures for ever, that nothing is unalterable, yet you have not been active in seeking to discover new truths. In short, my friend, you are a paradox.

B.   I suppose that an idea of where I am, of where I am not, is coming to me quite late in life. It is quite a complicated story. To start with, much of the research I have read has lacked involvement with the development activities of schools and colleges. There have been notable exceptions, such as Stenhouse (1973), but a large proportion of mainstream research has seemed impotent to me. This is why I have, until now, concerned myself with action through INSET activities, rather than research as a leading edge for development. The latter seemed to be an activity involving much flapping of wings but very little flying action.

F.   Yet you exhort your in-service students to do research; you even encourage, indeed require, that your PGCE (Post Graduate Certificate in Education) students do so. In this respect one might say that you are a downright hypocrite . . . a case of: 'do as I say, not as I do'!

B.   Yes, it has felt like that at times. But I've changed, perhaps because of supervising many of the dissertations done by these able students. I think that

behaviour is a function of experience; if our experience is destructive then so
will be our behaviour — on the other hand if one's experience is productive,
then . . . I guess that you are right; I have been something of a contradiction.
My discovery seems similar to the concept of 'I' as a living contradiction
discussed by Whitehead (1985b):

> . . . in the sense that I hold within myself, as a dialectical unity, mutually
> exclusive opposites of the form, I value freedom/I am negating freedom,
> or I value social justice/I am negating social justice. This experience of
> mutually exclusive values, moves me forward in a struggle to overcome
> the original experience in justice.

It is quite possible to avoid unpalatable truths about our professional self; for
example, we could avoid the issue, or deny the fact, or rationalise our position.
In the final analysis Polonius' advice to Laertes, although actually hollow in
the context of Shakespeare's *Hamlet*, offers good advice when honestly taken
on board:

> This above all, — to thine own self be true;

> And it must follow, as the night the day,

> Thou canst not then be false to any man.

F.   I see, you are saying that the notion of not doing research seems
incongruous with enabling others to do so?

B.   I think so, yes. Scientific research is a slippery concept, and can take on
such meaning as the user wishes to give it, but I now appreciate that research
can be useful in the practical sense; it may directly enhance the quality of
education in the activities of those engaged in the process. Therefore it is an
activity I value, and want to be involved in. But the learning that comes from
confronting myself is more wide-ranging than this . . .

F.   You have implied that you have a greater sense of where you are now
(and presumably where you are going). You have also hinted that this
experience of working with in-service students is not the only reason for this
change of direction.

B.   Right. I suppose that it's been a *gradual* process, when I think about it.
'When I think about it' is probably a key phrase! For years I have felt very
much like Edward Bear when he enters the world of Pooh Bear:

> Here is Edward Bear coming down stairs now, bump, bump, bump, on the back of his head . . . it is, as far as he knows, the only way of coming downstairs, but sometimes he feels that there really is another way, if only he could stop bumping for a moment and think about it. (Milne, 1958.)

I keep saying to my students that it is very important to create *intellectual space* in which to think. Teaching, in particular, is one of those occupations where work can become a bottomless pit of tasks and activities, unless time is carefully managed — yet it is a trap I seem to have fallen into myself . . .

Part of the problem may have to do with my enthusiasm. Most people would regard this as a positive virtue, but I think that unbridled enthusiasm can lead to one's concentration running wild towards the immediate task at hand — in my case, the year-to-year running of courses. This is not to say that my thinking has been stagnant; indeed if it had been I should have to concern myself with a more urgent introspection. No, I am a *facilitator of learning* rather than a teacher in the traditional sense of the term, and the two-way process of learning has also ensured *my* development. Yet, summoned by memos and notes, and bells (like Betjeman), I have concerned myself with the more immediate, rather than lift up my head to look around, and think more expansively. In retrospect this is something I very much regret.

F.   I see, so you put your absention from research down to a lack of time. If I were being provocative, I might say that was a neat excuse; one used by many, no doubt.

B.   I think a preoccupation with other tasks only partly sums up this self-imposed moratorium. The root cause probably lies deeper, and is likely to wear many faces.

F.   Hmm . . .

B.   I intimated earlier that much research related to education had the cutting edge of sponge; for a long time I questioned the *honesty* of much that I read about in some of the academic journals. Don't get me wrong, I'm not suggesting that their authors were anything but sincere and well intentioned. What I am trying to say is that their research did not speak the truth to me. These works seemed more concerned with statistics than sensitivities; rats rather than brats; research rather than the researched.

The situation I describe is complex and difficult to unravel. I suppose if I am honest part of it was tied closely to my sense of identity, my up-bringing in respect of research. Unfortunately, autonomy does not come easily because emotional links and ties are involved. You see, as a researcher, I was, until about 1982, socialised in a traditional household up on Quantitative Street (that is, apart from a period between 1970 and 1971, when I was too 'young' to notice). The truth is that the quantitative experience left me feeling cold. During this time I ostensibly learnt the skills of doing research, but even though I conducted some research as part of the process, I cannot say that I really researched. In the final analysis the activity was a hollow one for me; despite learning to speak the language of authoritarian social science, it did not help me to communicate with any audience of consequence.

I think it may help if I refer to some notes. Let me see, Reason & Marshall (1987) suggest that all good research is:

> for me, for us and for them: it speaks to three audiences, and contributes to each of these three areas of knowing. It is *for them* to the extent that it produces some kind of generalizable ideas and outcomes which elicit the response 'That's interesting' from those who are concerned to understand a similar field. It is *for us* to the extent that it responds to concerns of our praxis, is relevant and timely, and so produces the response 'That works!' from those who are struggling with problems in their field of action. It is *for me* to the extent that the process and outcomes respond directly to the individual teacher's being-in-the-world, and so elicits the response, 'That's exciting!' — taking exciting back to its root meaning, to set in action. Research thus contributes to personal motivation and development.

To my mind, I went around the track — but my efforts did not improve practice, nor so far as I am aware contribute to the body of knowledge, and I think the investment of time and effort promoted my own learning only marginally.

F.   You sound almost angry about it . . .?

B.   Looking back, I feel somehow cheated about not knowing the existence of other realities. Yes, initially a sense of disappointment inside, and later resentment, led me away from research. That diet of research I ate in Quantitative Street was so unpalatable to my taste that it resulted in a severe loss of appetite. People should not be socialised into having to eat only what is put on the table; there really ought to be a choice of menu. I agree with Rist (1977) when he said that issues of methodology are issues of strategy, not of morals.

To make matters worse, it is not easy to move away in order to get to what you do not know. In the short term it is easier, less painful, to stay the same. The sad fact is, my academic identity rested, in part, on the quantitative approach, therefore I think, sub-consciously, I had a vested interest in *not* questioning the validity of my own existence too closely. My intelligence cannot be applauded for 'playing the game', as Berne (1968) puts it. The truth is less flattering: caught up in the grip of a paradigm which I did not believe in, I must face up to the fact that in the final analysis the fault was mine. We are all technically free to think. There was nothing to stop the chap from Quantitative Street walking around and noticing how people lived elsewhere; recognising that a variety of food existed. This is what really hurts, the fact that I did not contemplate what might lie outside the world I found myself in. Sadly, my world at that time was not round. This voyage of discovery has been a tortured one; Eliot's words (T.S. not J.!) in Journey of the Magi, are very perceptive:

> ...... this Birth was
> Hard and bitter agony for us, like Death, our death.

The truth is that I was not as aware as I should have been of alternative approaches to research in education. Looking back, I am mortified at the fact that in 1973, Entwhistle, for example, writing for the Open University was making intellectually stimulating statements like:

> As far as educational research is concerned, the paradigm of the hypothetico-deductive method is an ideal rarely achieved. The complexity of children's behaviour in a classroom often leaves research workers still at the stage of hypothesis hunting . . . Science provides important guidelines, but there is the uneasy realisation that social science may, after all, be different in kind from natural science.

Why was my reading so narrow, my perspective so myopic in 1977, when, for example, Magoon was expressing a growing concern that 'there are some good indications that educational research may have reached a crisis stage with regard to its major Fisherian experimental design tradition'. Nearly a decade later, and thanks in part to an ongoing dialogue with an external examiner, I had begun to open my eyes. When I looked I began to see. Reading books like Burgess (1985) helped to demystify how research is actually done by other people in educational settings; this made me feel real. Today, I read and I understand. I have discovered that the words of Elton and Laurillard (1979) accorded with those already writ large within me, but which for so long remained unarticulated, buried in the safety of my subconscious:

> The traditional research paradigm in education . . . has been culled from the physical sciences. It involves the analysis of complicated situations into component parts, followed by the controlled variation of single variables leading to a better understanding of each separate part, and

finally the reassembly of the parts into the original whole with increased understanding. This essentially reductionist approach has been immensely successful in fundamental physics; much less so in its applications, where it has not been possible to analyse situations in terms of a small number of independent variables.

F.   Painful it may have been, but nevertheless it sounds as if real learning has taken place, Barrie. It's all grist for the mill surely?

B.   True, but I think it has been unnecessarily slow, and very much a 'chance occurrence' as they would say. Despite realising that for me at least, a method of investigation which claimed the power confidently to predict and/ or prove or reject truths about human beings on the strength of applying 'statistical treatments' to data, gathered in a mechanical way about 'subjects', and in a context often located outside the reality of school life, often did not seem appropriate — I failed to stop and question the prevailing orthodoxy. I think my great failing was that I did not step outside the established frame of reference, to question, to reflect on what I intuitively felt.

Thankfully, I now feel empowered, autonomous, a frame of mind similar to that thoughtfully put by Keane (1987): 'I finally learned to accept my experience as a valid source of knowledge. I broke through the cultural conditioning which had me conceive of myself as a derivative learner. I perceived myself as learner in a new way. This insight was an important shift . . .' I do not believe that one must of necessity experience pain in order to learn. The essential requirement is freedom; 'freedom to learn' as Rogers (1983) puts it. I think that a choice of paradigm for any research project is something that ought to rest firmly with the individual. The function of institutions of learning is to provide the conceptual tools and skills which, when set in the context of a critical community of friends, help a person make decisions in the light of circumstances. Eclecticism Rules — O.K! No research paradigm should be reified and treated as sacrosanct, otherwise there lies the danger that we may wish to convert others to our way of thinking. With apologies to T.S. Eliot, his words, turned upside down and used in a context for which they were not meant, seem a poignant reminder of this:

> We returned to our places, these Kingdoms,
> But no longer at ease here, in the old dispensation,
> With an alien people clutching their gods.
> I should be glad of another death.

A fundamental truth portrayed in a lighter vein by Nisbet (1980), takes the form of an imaginative report of a fictional advisory council in 1810 asked to forecast the development of the transport system:

'One thing' they concluded, 'has stood the test of time over several thousand years: the horse has come to stay. Authorities as diverse as Ghengis Khan, Dick Turpin, Julius Caesar, and Buffalo Bill, all agree on one thing, from long experience, that there is no better way of getting from one place to another than on a horse.'

This wise counsel reminds us that defending positions (and by implication vested interests) *vis-à-vis* the hypothetico-deductive and naturalistic approaches is unhelpful, and argues instead for the emergence of a spectrum of research styles.

A Born Again Researcher?

F. The Magi apparently have not been the only ones to travel; you seem to have covered much ground too. One might say that (tongue in cheek!) you are a born again researcher . . .

B. It's certainly a relief to be moving forward; standing still can be very tiring! I think that the spur for wishing to research was a feeling that as teaching practice supervisor, my work had acquired a character of conscientious routine. I decided that the honest thing to do would be to investigate my own practice. I confronted the tension between my actual and potential performance, and I resolved to intervene, actively, in order to improve things.

F. Talk and action are a long way apart. What are you doing about this?

B. Guiding me are some overriding principles which accord with my value system. These have helped me to develop a methodology. Let me try and explain these to you. I believe that it is more worthwhile to listen than to list; that the emphasis ought to be on learning rather than on laying down the law, and I agree with Gadamer (1975) that formulating a question is more important than concentrating on being able to give an answer. The following may help to convey some of my thinking:

'First of all', he said, 'if you can learn a simple trick scout, you'll get along a lot better with all kinds of folks. You never really understand a person until you consider things from his point of view.'

'Sir?'. . .

'Until you climb into his skin and walk around in it.'

This extract from Harper Lee's *To Kill a Mockingbird* illustrates my belief about understanding social situations. Rist (1977) linking this principle to the research context, argues that all knowledge is social. That reasoning makes sense to me, and if Rist is correct, it underlines the value of linking research to the way people construe reality.

You see, I believe that educational research should wear a human face. A comment (source not disclosed) referred to by Cohen & Manion (1980) strikes a melodious chord to me 'for scientific purposes, treat people as if they were human beings'. We need to talk with one another, and not march over people in a clinical search for answers to hypotheses (often conceived far from the richness and colour, and heat, of school/college life!). '. . . ignoring or negating the internal world of people misses the essence of their personhood, flattens human reality and leads to educational practices which are mechanistic and lacking in respect for the basic integrity of the other person' (Pope, Gilbert & Watts, 1983).

In retrospect I can see that a bad case of conceptual rigor mortis prevented me from seeing the relevance of a constructive approach to educational research. Despite being introduced to the work of George Kelly in 1970, and subsequently using Kelly's ideas in school, I'm afraid that for some reason I left my constructive goggles in the case when it came to research! A matter of creating a false dichotomy between teaching and researching. Now I appreciate that it is not a matter of choice — an either/or situation, and I agree with the Frankfurt school, that the two may very usefully be one (See Kelly, 1955; 1969).

F.   George Kelly?

B.   George Kelly's creative theory holds that reality is not a universal thing: that each person constructs his/her own reality. Depending on a person's experiences, intelligence, self system, cognitive style etc., the way ideas and events are construed will be different. Different, that is, to a greater or lesser extent, so that people who are socialised in similar ways may construe events in broadly similar ways, whilst people who have widely different experiences may be more likely to view things differently. Yet, each person will see the world in a unique way. As an emergent researcher I found the following extract from Kelly, quoted by Pope *et al.* (1983), useful in gathering together my thoughts when contemplating the choice of an appropriate research methodology:

We assume that all our present interpretations of the universe are subject to revision or replacement. We have to understand that there are always some alternative constructions available to choose among in dealing with the world . . . We call this philosophical position constructive alternativism.

Like the extract from *To Kill A Mockingbird*, this suggests that an important thing to do might be to attempt to get on the inside of the other's thinking; to take on board their perspective at the very least and at best to empathise with them. As Kelly (1969), also referred to by Pope *et al.*, puts it: 'the ultimate explanation of human behaviour lies in examining man's undertakings, the questions he asks, the lines of enquiry he initiates, the strategies he employs rather than analysing the logical pattern and impact of the event with which he collides.' A point which Kelly feels strongly about: 'I am very sceptical of any piece of human research in which the subject's questions and contributions have not been elicited or have been ignored in the final analysis of results.'

F.   It's all very well wanting to get on the inside of the other's thinking, but from what you say, each person will think differently about issues. Will that help you?

B.   That is just a starting point; a means to an end. My aim is to promote collaboration between participants on a status-equal basis, as far as learning is concerned. Rather than treading along well trodden-paths (HMI, 1982), rather than dictating the character of teaching practice from college, I resolved that the way forward was to explore with other participants how it might be. Much educational research has emanated from the perspective(s) of the researcher; what I call the *leading construct*. However, this type of construct or hypothesis, derived from the researcher's perspective, runs the risk of turning the research process into a *fact-finding* or *testing* one, rather than a *learning* orientated process. Stimulated by an article written by Boud & Griffin (1987), my aim is to facilitate learning amongst participants:

> Much work on adult learning has derived from the perspective of teachers or researchers: they enter the world of learners with their own concerns and investigate matters which they believe to be important. This sometimes leads to important findings, but often these do not communicate well to those of us who are learners as well as teachers. It is not simply a matter of the way in which this research is expressed; it is the way in which it is conceived. If we wish to benefit from research then at least some of it must adopt the learner's frame of reference: it must address the concerns which they think are important and respect their felt experience.

F.   This explains why you emphasise the importance of collaboration, but you seem to be wanting more than just collaboration. If your collaborators are to be effective participants in the research, you will have to monitor the nature of that participation carefully.

B.   Sure. I am interested in facilitating the release of creative energy between people; listening and talking at depth, with fellow human beings who are participants in this undertaking. I have faith that this will enable us to learn from one another.

F.   But do your values lead to a *disciplined* approach associated with proper research?

B.   I see myself in the process of becoming an action researcher. Action research has been established as a disciplined form of research. The seminal work of Lewin (1946), along with other works, for example, Stenhouse (1975), Elliott (1979), Nixon (1981), Carr & Kemmis (1986), have been influential in this respect. It was recently reassuring to read a definition quoted by Whitehead (1986), because it read like a description of the research I have started to initiate:

> Educational action research is a term used to describe a family of activities in curriculum development, professional development, school involvement programs, and systems planning and policy development. These activities have in common the identification of strategies of planned action which are implemented, and then systematically submitted to observation, reflection and change. Participants in the action being considered are integrally involved in all of these activities.

I think that Whitehead sharpens the focus, and helps to cut through to the kernel of the activity: 'There are two essential aims of all action research activity: to improve and to involve'; and suggests what he considers to be essential features of the process:

> . . . firstly a project takes as its subject-matter a social practice, regarding it as a strategic action susceptible of improvement; secondly, the project proceeds through a spiral of cycles of planning, acting, observing and reflecting, with each of these activities being systematically and self-critically implemented and interrelated; thirdly, the project involves those responsible for the practice in each of the moments of the activity, widening participation in the project gradually to include others affected by the practice, and maintaining collaborative control of the process.

F.   But where is the *discipline* of proper research?

B.   The approach I am adopting *is* a disciplined one, and I shall try to outline it. I do think, however, that provocative comments (whether unintentional or intentional) like 'proper research' are unhelpful, because they may inhibit the very stuff of which social research is made: free and open debate.

In order to answer your question, I must point out that working within a holistic framework means that a systematic approach is essential; it would be impossible to survive without it! I agree with Parlett & Hamilton (1976), that the school/college context is too complex for a preconceived research design to be appropriate. Elton & Laurillard (1979) sum the point up well:

> They (Parlett and Hamilton) suggest a methodology that takes account of this complexity by allowing the focus of the evaluation to develop as the study proceeds, rather than in advance of it. Thus those aspects of the context that are important for explaining student behaviour are less likely to be neglected.

But this does not mean that discipline is not required, although it may be different in kind from that which is traditionally associated with research in educational contexts.

Similarly, another obstacle which may temporarily obscure the fact that my preferred approach is disciplined, hinges on the assumption that all research must concern itself with cause and effect. Again, Elton & Laurillard (1979) tackle this matter when they say:

> what it is important to study is not so much things and events by themselves, but the relationship and — in more complicated instances — systems of relationships between them. This shift in attention, from events to relations, has happened in a number of the sciences in the past half century . . .

Because my research project has a different philosophical base from that of the traditional research paradigm in education, existing criteria associated with rigour, whilst providing useful questions to address, may need to be reappraised. New wine requires new wine skins! I agree with Guba (1978) when he says that concepts like validity, reliability and objectivity are in need of reinterpretation in order to be fully applicable to naturalistic enquiry. Thus Guba suggests: 'intrinsic adequacy in lieu of internal validity, extrinsic adequacy in lieu of external validity or generalizability, replicability in lieu of reliability, and impartiality in lieu of objectivity . . .' Let's take validity as an example. House (1977) suggests that:

> Validity is provided by cross-checking different data sources and by testing perceptions against those of participants. Issues and questions arise from the people and situations being studied rather than the investigator's perceptions. Concepts and indicators 'derive from the

subject's world of meaning and action'. In constructing explanations, the naturalist looks for convergence of his data sources and develops sequential, phase-like explanations that assume no event has single causes. Working backwards from an important event is a common procedure. Introspection is a common source of data.

My approach is disciplined because I am taking care to check the information by using the strategy of *triangulation*, defined by Cohen & Manion (1980) as:

> the use of two or more methods of data collection in the study of some aspect of human behaviour. . . . The use of multiple methods, or the multi-method approach as it is sometimes called, contrasts with the ubiquitous but generally more vulnerable single-methods approach that characterises so much of research in the social sciences.

In this respect my research techniques include, amongst others: semi-structured discussions; agenda-setting group discussions; fixed role character sketches.

Another way in which my research is disciplined is that I take care to validate any claims made about meaning, through negotiation with fellow participants. This means, for example, establishing informal validating support sets and using more formal sets such as the School Experience Committee within the Faculty.

F.   There is a consistency to your argument. But I wonder if there is a chance that you have been dominated by the seductive qualities of what you have read?

B.   Becoming more informed about possibilities through reading is only part of it; action is another. The process of self-reflection in which I am engaging was helped along by my active involvement, as tutor, in the systematic course-evaluation procedures that now form an integral part of our PGCE programme. Since 1984 when Lomax introduced the process of critical evaluation to the Faculty it has become an essential part of my professional make-up (see Lomax & McLeman, 1984). My current research interest is to broaden the focus of this evaluation work and build a definite focus for action into it. An important principle of action research is that it starts small.

This has been made possible by new developments in the organisation of the PGCE school experience programme. The Faculty has decided to move towards a new partnership arrangement with schools whereby an even greater emphasis is placed on the teacher's role in student supervision. Under this scheme, designated teachers will become paid, school-based supervisors. My project seeks to improve the quality of postgraduate education, for students following the secondary (11–18) option, by getting all involved to work together on improving the quality of their experience on T.P. (Teaching Practice). This means college tutors, teachers, PGCE students, and school pupils all collaborating together.

F.   Where do you start?

B.   The starting point must be how things *are* for people. Individual discussions can be formative in the sense that they enable participants to reflect on their practice. It then becomes possible to facilitate a dialogue between the holders of these various versions of reality. This negotiation is gradually leading to a shared sense of meaning. In this way, we all have a platform from which to speak; together, we are evaluating and acting to improve our practice . . . it's an important ongoing process.

F.   So the living contradiction has generated the energy to turn theory into practice!

B.   I would say generated the energy to create theory from practice.

Further Adventures in the Wild Woods?

In this chapter, I have tried to investigate my own learning as a researcher. The experience has been a very sobering one for me.

Recognising a sense of tension that existed in my thoughts concerning the quality of conscientious routine that was characterising my work, I confronted myself as I had become — and resolved to deal with what Whitehead (1985b) called the 'I as a living contradiction'. In order to proceed, I had to find a relevant way of exploring this area of work. My thinking led me to a smouldering rag-bag of reasons for not believing in the power of research to promote change at the 'chalk face'.

My current experience of 'the research world' has widened my view of what educational research may be. The warm and facilitating, yet critical, face of adult learning at the University of Surrey has created a new excitement within me about the challenge surrounding learning. My introduction to the British Educational Research Association (BERA) has also given me the confidence to embark upon a dialogue with others within a wider learning community. Rogers' (1983) concept of freedom to learn is an important one, and in direct contrast to that of paternalism. Like Mole's journey into the Wild Woods, it has reminded me that facilitating learning is the same in any context:

He [Badger] sat in his arm chair at the head of the table, and nodded gravely at intervals as the animals told their story; and he did not seem surprised or shocked at anything, and he never said, 'I told you so', or, 'Just what I always said', or remarked that they ought to have done so-and-so, or ought not to have done something else. The Mole began to feel very friendly towards him.

In this context I think that BERA has a crucial role to play in encouraging others to understand the benefits and challenges that the Wild Woods hold for them. The conditions for open thinking, for academic freedom from *within* as well as *without*, should be ensured. Mole's new-found friend would agree:

'The Wild Wood is pretty well populated by now; with all the usual lot, good, bad, and indifferent — I name no names. It takes all sorts to make a world. But I fancy you know something about them yourself by this time.'

'I do indeed,' said the Mole, with a light shiver.

'Well, well,' said the Badger, patting him on the shoulder, 'it was your first experience of them, you see. They're not so bad really; and we must all live and let live. But I'll pass the word round to-morrow, and I think you'll have no further trouble. Any friend of mine walks where he likes in this country, or I'll know the reason why!'

Part II:

Bringing about change in schools

6 Bringing about gender equality of opportunity in a special school

KATE BURTON

This report is an account and evaluation of an action management project which was undertaken in a special school. It chronicles and reflects upon the events of a year and a half during which time I attempted to highlight and reform attitudes to gender issues within the school in which I was working. I sought to open a debate on gender issues within the school, introduce a policy of equal opportunities, bring about some organisational changes to reduce sex stereotyping, and as a result of this work, to reflect upon the development of my own managerial skills.

The early sections provide the reader with background information about the school and set the study in the wider context of research into gender issues. The major part of the chapter reports upon the methods used and the results of the enquiry. The final section analyses the outcome of the project and the ways in which change was achieved. Through my struggle to identify and come to terms with my own management style I was able to draw some more general observations and have a greater understanding of the role of headteacher.

As a newly appointed deputy headteacher I was naturally interested in and concerned about the development of my own leadership skills. In order to monitor my own progress and growth as a manager I decided to focus on just one aspect of the manager's many-faceted role, managing change. The area I chose to highlight and reform within the school was attitudes to gender issues. The problems associated with gender issues permeate our society and are detrimental both to the individual's self-development and the individual's contribution to society. Schools tend to exacerbate matters by reinforcing sex segregations and stereotyping. This discrimination exaggerates the negative aspects of sex roles, denying children choice and stultifying their growth. Through debate and negotiation I wished to formulate a policy for equal opportunities and to alter practice within the school by initiating a programme of reform. By carefully analysing this change I hoped to gain an insight into my own practice by examining and reflecting upon the development of my management skills.

I was working in a school for children with moderate learning difficulties. It is a mixed school with an age range of 5-16 years. There are currently 126 pupils on roll but the school could accommodate as many as 160 children and is classified as a group 7S (A DES classification which determines school establishment based on pupil numbers). There are 12 teachers, one headteacher and four ancillary staff. The problems of falling rolls and the uncertainty caused by the local education authority's review of special school provision has affected the school adversely. During the course of this project a new headteacher was appointed, the previous incumbent having founded the school some 28 years ago. In addition the school is involved in the new technical and vocational education extension and this will mean major changes taking place in the next five years. Inevitably these factors have had some bearing on the progress and development of the project.

I first visited the school as a prospective candidate for the deputy headship in June 1986. A startling feature of the school was the fact that senior pupils were segregated according to sex for all lessons. When I took up my appointment in January 1987 I quickly learned that sexism was rife.

'Sexism is a term meaning stereotyping people by sex, just as racism is stereotyping people by race'. (Delamont, 1980). This sexism was implicitly built into the school curriculum through which we were grooming the girls in 'female occupations', fitting them to be housewives and mothers, whilst the boys, with a heavy commitment to craft, design and technology (CDT), were learning to be wage earners as semi-skilled labourers. The boys did some cooking and attended one health education lesson once a week which dealt with basic sex education using television programmes and videos. They did not join the girls for child care, sewing or general home skills lessons. The girls did no CDT and very little science. Social relationships between boys and girls were bizarre. Since opportunities for normal interactions within the classroom were scarce the pupils were deeply entrenched in stereotyped relationships and behaviour, which led to wild flamboyant displays during playtimes. The headteacher was an unashamed male chauvinist. He held traditional values, girls should be girls and boys should be boys. No females, staff or children, were allowed to wear trousers to school. He often referred to his female staff as his 'bevy of beauties' and difficult girls were 'hussies'. Male members of staff, three excluding the headteacher, seldom came into contact with the girls, who were an enigma to them. They did not even know the girls' names. The second deputy, a male, actually told me quite bluntly that he did not teach girls. I had set myself a seemingly impossible task. However, there were some positive aspects and glimmers of hope. The female members of staff were well aware of the inequalities and many, I later discovered, shared my view that some things should change. In addition, junior children in the school were mixed, sharing all lessons and experiences. It was generally agreed that this department in the school was lively, stimulating and successful.

Education and Sexism

It is 40 years since the United Nations formulated the Universal Declaration of Human Rights and yet nations, sects, groups and individuals are still victimised or discriminated against every day; sometimes intentionally as the direct result of hatred or bigotry, often unintentionally as a result of unfounded prejudice, ignorance, neglect or oversight. People can become living contradictions, espousing one set of ideals and yet living out contradictory values. We are often unconscious of the inconsistency of our behaviour, oblivious of the meaning implicit in our actions. We are socially constructed beings embedded in our history and traditions. Radical thinkers fighting oppression threaten our equilibrium by demanding that we rationalise our behaviour, and as a result they are often pilloried. The Women's Liberation Movement has been just such a group in recent years. They have challenged the traditional role of women in our society, presenting powerful arguments for change and reappraisal. Ann Oakley posed the fundamental questions; 'Everybody knows that men and women are different. But behind this knowledge lies a certain uneasiness: how different are they? What is the extent of the difference? What significance does it have for the way male and female behave and are treated in society?' (Oakley, 1972).

Male supremacy has been a feature of our society for centuries. Women, it has been alleged, are physically, intellectually and psychologically weaker than men, well fitted to the nurturing role for which nature has biologically determined them. Furthermore, to many researchers, women have been invisible, regarded only in terms of male behaviour and therefore deviant. Researchers have tended 'to regard male behaviour as the "norm" and female behaviour as some kind of deviation from that norm. Thus when women do not conform to the standards of psychological expectation, the conclusion has generally been that something is wrong with women' (Gilligan, 1987). These views are clearly flawed. Women are different, not substandard. They have many different roles and share many qualities with men. Not all women conform to the idealised feeble little woman so dependent upon the men in her life for economic, emotional and spiritual support. Working-class and black women have always been expected to labour long and hard, physical and emotional strength a sheer necessity in their everyday lives as they struggle to support their families. During times of crisis like war, women often take on 'men's jobs', becoming farmers, factory workers and heavy goods drivers. As women have gained access to higher education time and again they have proved themselves to be the intellectual equals of men. A woman's role, personality and intellectual capability are clearly diverse; she is not limited to a stereotyped image. The cross-cultural studies of Margaret Mead in the 1920s and 1930s support this view. She discovered so many types of masculinity and femininity amongst the tribes she studied that she refuted the concept of a universal 'masculine' or 'feminine' personality, totally undermining our system of sex stereotypes (Mead, 1950).

However, our society has flourished upon sex stereotyping, especially the sexual division of labour — woman the homemaker, man the bread winner. 'That a woman's place is at home looking after husband and children is a myth which helps to validate the continued cheap reproduction of workers and therefore, the maintenance of capitalist business and industry' (Sharpe, 1976). It has been argued that to change the status quo would cause unhappiness and tragedy, destroying family life, the bedrock of our society; but surely it is sex stereotyping which leads to unhappiness and an indefensible waste of talent.

> The implications of both male and female ideals and stereotypes are not beneficial to those striving to follow them. For women, following the stereotype can lead to self-sacrifice and an implicit acceptance of inferiority. For men, the active pursuit of ambition can consume their lives and destroy intimate relationships with other people, especially women and children. (Sharpe, 1976).

If we want society to improve and become more just and egalitarian, if we want to embrace the United Nations Declaration of Human Rights, we must move away from stereotypes and assume that any human characteristic is cultural and hence open to change, education being one means through which change can be achieved.

In 1967 the United Nations passed the following resolution: 'All appropriate measures shall be taken to ensure to girls and women, married or unmarried, equal rights with men in education at all levels.' Equality of opportunity is now enshrined in government directives and new education initiatives like technical and vocational education, but the world of education is slow to respond. Of course, it is wrong to generalise. Some local education authorities are actively endorsing positive gender policies and initiatives, appointing special advisers and publishing helpful material to enable teachers to become more aware of gender issues. However, many schools throughout the country are still governed by the thinking and beliefs of the 1960s which were exemplified in the Crowther Report: 'It is true that there is a broad distinction between boys' and girls' interests which is rightly reflected in curriculum planning' (Crowther Committee, 1959, para 170). Some schools seem to enforce a set of sex and gender roles which are even more rigid than those current in the wider society. Daily class and school routines and methods of organisation constantly remind children that they are either male or female, and curriculum subjects are traditionally perceived by pupils and staff as more suitable for one particular sex. Sexism is implicit in teachers' attitudes and pupil/teacher relationships. Stereotyped images are also portrayed in teaching materials as is so well demonstrated in this spoof quoted by Sara Delamont;

> See John kick a football. See Jane help mummy with the dishes. See John paddle in the water. See Jane watch from the beach. See John suggest an adventure. See Jane tag obediently along behind. See John grow into a mature person . . . See Jane, on the other hand, grow up to be a right little weed. (Delamont, 1980.)

The school in which I was working was certainly guilty of all these sins. It was organised around the differences rather than the similarities between the sexes, encouraging polarity between the extremes of masculinity and femininity. To me, a liberal feminist, they were glaringly blatant, to many of my colleagues they were just part of their everyday lives. The school had existed unchanged for so long that people had ceased to question and evaluate what was happening. I decided to start asking questions and formulated the following aims:

— to open a debate on gender issues in the school;

— to draw up a policy document on equal opportunities;

— to widen options for all pupils;

— to provide opportunities for male members of staff to teach the girls;

— to provide opportunities for boys and girls to be taught together;

— ultimately to introduce complete integration.

Undertaking a research project for the first time is a daunting prospect. It seems hidebound by jargon and awesome practices such as statistical analysis, systematic investigations and the establishment and testing of hypotheses and principles. It is apparently the province of the intellectual elite who propose and validate their theories which are then handed down to the more menial practitioners to enrich and improve their practice. However, many teachers are sceptical of educational research and resist or doubt its findings. Indeed, empirical study, whilst aiming to produce scientific, value-free results, is not always the objective, methodic approach it purports to be. As Pamela Lomax (1986a) says; 'The idea that particular research paradigms are based on identifiable value positions is not a new one'. Researchers can also find that as observers they lack the background knowledge which could help them comprehend classroom interaction, so there is a strong case for teachers to lose their inhibitions and prejudices and adopt the role of researcher themselves. However, to criticise some aspects of applied research is not to deny its value or to denigrate its contribution to educational theory. It is merely research on a larger scale than most teachers would wish to undertake, its purpose being to establish relationships and test theories.

> An alternative method of research is called action research. Action research is a form of self-reflective enquiry undertaken by participants in social (including educational) situations in order to improve the rationality and justice of (a) their own social or educational practices, (b) their understanding of these practices and (c) the situations in which these practices are carried out. (Kemmis & Henry, 1984.)

This method of research is not without its critics: 'Such research is derided as particularistic and over subjective' (Lomax, 1986a). However, the need for open dialogue and co-operation between practitioners and researchers is undeniable:

> It is to adopt a dialectical perspective which recognises that schools can no more change without the informed commitment of teachers than teachers can change without the informed commitment of the institutions in which they work, that schools and systems are similarly interdependent and interactive in the process of reform, and that education can only be reformed by reforming the practices that constitute it. (Kemmis, 1985a)

The critical factor in deciding upon a research method is to establish the purpose of the research. Applied or empirical research was wholly inappropriate for my project; I needed a method of research which would be much more specific to my particular needs. I needed help to record and analyse what happened and needed to be able to examine my own intervention and reactions. I needed a method that would help me to collect data, analyse and reflect upon the information and draw conclusions which would enable me to improve my own practice. I needed to understand what was going on, to use what Wright Mills (1976) called the sociological imagination: 'The sociological imagination I remind you, in considerable part consists of the capacity to shift from one perspective to another and in the process to build up an adequate view of a total society and its components.' I therefore chose the action research paradigm without hesitation. Unlike applied research it could contribute directly to the solutions of problems; its emphasis is not so much on obtaining generalisable scientific knowledge as on precise knowledge for a particular situation and purpose.

My specific problem was how I was going to manage and effect change within my own school. I did not want to construct meta-educational theory; I merely wanted to formulate my own personal theories on school management and determine how I might in time become an effective and efficient headteacher. Within the theory of action research I found both the means of recording data, the research diary or learning log, and the process of evaluation, the self-reflective spiral. I used a research diary extensively and soon acquired the habit of writing down the day's happenings, conversations, discussions and decisions. I recorded staff meetings myself but also asked another member of staff to minute these meetings so I had the added input of a different perspective. I gradually involved my colleagues in my project and invited their comments and observations. This collaboration not only helped the development of the project and cemented professional relationships but also provided valuable alternative views and observations.

The process of action research involves a spiral process of planning, acting, observing systematically, reflecting and returning to the next planning stage. Periodically I sifted through my entries and records, attempting to identify key elements and events and analysing responses. This form of reflexivity was invaluable and provided a deeper understanding of the task, of colleagues and children but most of all myself. I find I agree wholeheartedly with Stenhouse (1975) that action research provides 'a capacity for autonomous professional development through systematic self study'. Furthermore, as Kemmis (1985a) says: 'Self evaluation was the basis for — the sine qua non of — educational innovation and change.'

The Action

I would like to present my action as six cycles of planning, acting and reflecting.

1.   *Plan*: My initial impressions led me to believe the school was organised in a way which precluded equal opportunities for all pupils. I therefore decide to embark upon a fact-finding mission.

Action: I listen and talk to colleagues informally to discover their feelings and the reasons for the structure of the organisation.

Observations/reflections: I discover that people are largely supportive, unaware of the injustices in the present system but wary of change. However progress is hindered by the 'testing games' of colleagues as we all adjust to each other and establish a new pecking order. In due course I formulate my aims.

2.   *Plan*: I form the following strategy to achieve my aims: (a) to convince the headteacher of the need for equal opportunities; (b) to convince other members of staff that change is possible/desirable.

Action: I discuss equal opportunities with the headteacher, seizing every opportunity to reinforce my argument. As the father of two successful girls, one a nurse and the other training to be a solicitor, he is reasonably receptive. From staff discussions at staff meetings we formulate the following policy statement:

> We believe in equality of opportunity for all pupils at this school. Pupils should have the opportunity to develop their talents and interests. There should be the capacity to make choices, information on which to base preferences and a climate of tolerance in which to explore alternatives.

This battle is won somewhat easily due to the timely inclusion of the school in plans for the county's technical and vocational education submission to the training commission which, of course, makes equality of opportunity obligatory.

Observations/reflections: Due to concerns expressed by several members of staff, especially the craft teacher who has seen reports of research which suggests that girls do not flourish in his subject when working alongside boys, it is decided to proceed gradually. We look at relevant research and monitor proceedings carefully.

3.   *Plan*: A plan of action was devised taking the above objections into consideration, so as to acclimatise staff and pupils slowly to changes.

Action: The girls begin CDT lessons and the boys begin needlework in the guise of upholstery; these are single-sex lessons. A few girls are infiltrated into the nature club to work alongside boys with the teacher who had claimed not to teach girls.

Observations/reflections: The boys love sewing and some are now proudly making teddy bears! The girls dislike CDT and revel in the novelty of a male teacher, playing all kinds of wicked testing games. Support is needed and given to the craft teacher who resolves to find more interesting work for the girls. Other female members of staff collaborate to improve the girls' attitude to CDT. Things gradually improve and one or two of the girls begin to show real talent. Nature club is successful due to the enthusiasm for the subject — no one really notices the changes. I decide we are ready to take the next step.

4.   *Plan*: I begin to work on the next stage of my plan, full integration of all pupils.

Action: I draw up class lists for September 1987. I reorganise the school in four different ways, one of which is total integration. My purpose in doing this is to stimulate discussion amongst the staff. My own feeling is that full integration should take place later, after the present senior pupils, who have really entrenched sex stereotyped ideas, leave. I want change to be successful when it happens and feel we should work towards this by integrating the middle school first.

Observations/reflections: I discuss the lists with the headteacher who expresses interest but basically resists such fundamental changes. He is due to retire and understandably wants the school to remain as it is. He wisely counsels that the new headteacher should be the one to make such major changes. I agree but want to start discussions in order to lay the foundations for change. I ask to be allowed to show the lists to other members of staff in order to gauge their reactions. The headteacher is puzzled at this suggestion and feels that such decisions should be made by senior management and are not the concern of the class teacher. I show the lists to key members of staff anyway and receive a great deal of support. Other people come up with alternative suggestions and become more approachable and willing to talk. However, we all decide that any major changes must wait for the new headteacher.

5.   *Plan*: I discuss reorganisation plans with the new headteacher. She is very supportive and keen to initiate change and reform. She becomes a potent force in the project. A new member of staff is appointed and it is decided that he should spearhead changes.

Action: The new member of staff is a drama teacher and very keen on team teaching (so is the new headteacher). Mixed drama lessons and team teaching is introduced. It is planned to integrate the middle school after Easter and class lists are drawn up.

Observations/reflections: The Spring term is a dismal failure. There are personality clashes between the staff and behaviour problems with the pupils. The experiment is abandoned and it is decided not to integrate the middle school classes due to staff changes and general upheaval caused by technical and vocational education (TVE) pressures and courses.

6.   *Plan*: The headteacher decides to impose a deadline for total integration: September 1988.

Action: I draw up class lists for discussion at the next staff meeting. This is a 'fiasco'. There is no discussion on integration and the meeting degenerates into an argument between different factions within the school.

Present position: Integration will happen in September but without the discussion that I thought was so vital. It has become a *fait accompli*. Everyone knows the headteacher's views and is unwilling to give the matter any further consideration. There will be many other changes in September, four new members of staff and a completely new timetable to comply with TVE demands, so integration palls to insignificance.

Analysis

Initially the project proceeded slowly but steadily. My first real revelation was a confirmation of the concept of living contradictions. There was genuine surprise, astonishment and even consternation when individuals realised the injustices in the school's organisation. The school had functioned in much the same way for more than 20 years; people had ceased to question why they did things. The organisation had taken on a life of its own. Educational practices were enshrined in the protective phrase: 'That's the way we do it here'. It led colleagues to say things like 'but I don't teach girls' without seeing the true import of what they were saying. After I had made everyone aware of our actions by articulating the hidden aims of our curriculum, i.e. girls would work in the home and boys would be the bread winners (which is clearly inappropriate in 1988) there was a consensus of opinion that things should change. The policy document was adopted unanimously and even with a degree of self-satisfaction. However, there was a fundamental resistance to actual change. People were comfortable and were quick to find reasons for postponing taking action. There was undoubtedly also an element of fear. 'Will I be able to cope with change?' was clearly visible on several faces.

A major lesson learnt from my project was that change becomes less of a threat if it is small, well planned and eventually successful. The widening of the curriculum for all pupils proved to be beneficial. All children began to produce work of which they were proud. Working together to achieve definite aims also improved relationships within the staff-room. Petty jealousies were forgotten as colleagues earnestly discussed the girls' bad behaviour in craft lessons and came up with positive suggestions of help. This was a new departure in a staff-room where the accepted opinion (emanating from the headteacher) was that if teachers could not control a class they were no good!

Another clear message was that class teachers do want to be included in policy making and decision taking. They grow in stature and confidence when their opinion is sought and valued. It is a waste of human resources to disregard the valuable contribution that all members of staff can make to an organisation.

Looking back at the records of the project provides a salutary lesson in the management of change. With the advent of the new headteacher there were too many changes heaped on pupils and staff. Many of the changes were poorly or hastily planned and resulted in disaster. There were numerous staff absences during this period, which I believe to be a clear indication of stress and a degree of demoralisation. Although I am well aware of the ways in which disaffected or antagonistic members of staff can block change, I still see the setting of a deadline only as a last resort. In this situation it clearly stifled any further discussion, and although the ultimate aim of the project was achieved it was a somewhat hollow victory.

Conclusion

I am happy to report that I have achieved some improvement in the school situation. Sexism is no longer a striking organisational feature of the school. Pupils are discovering new talents, working alongside each other in harmony and beginning to revise their stereotyped views of the opposite sex. Teachers are also more egalitarian. I conclude this to be a beneficial outcome of my action research project.

The project has also increased my understanding of the nature of organisations. The school was run as a club culture. Class teachers had few real responsibilities; all decisions had to be approved by the headteacher. The result was exactly that described by Handy (1984): 'If the organization is so regimented or so distrustful that all controls are before-the-event then it is unlikely to be very progressive, very exciting or very successful.' The school also lacked clear structure, and 'Structure is a means for attaining the objectives and goals of an organisation' (Child, 1984). I believe it is essential to develop a structure in a school, to allocate people and resources to tasks and to provide the mechanisms for co-ordinating the tasks, i.e. job descriptions and working parties. There should be a clear system for decision making and responsibilities should be assigned and respected. It is vital to set goals and to have a means of evaluating the people and work within the organisation.

I now have a greater understanding of the task of effecting change. Organisations can become so powerful that they take on a life of their own and become resistant to change. The organisational and material structure of the institutions in which we work constrain our educational actions and practices, thereby limiting innovation and development. To effect change is therefore a real challenge. There must be a clearly defined goal, a carefully considered plan of action and a means of reflecting on and analysing results; rather like an action research spiral. Indeed my project did bring about change. We had a goal to work towards, namely equal opportunities. There was an increase in interests and debate as we planned our strategies and as a staff we began to evaluate our work. I managed to achieve the participation of my colleagues; we began the process of self-evaluation and as a result became a critical community. We therefore achieved freedom from institutional constraints and began to act deliberately.

Undoubtedly I also have a greater understanding of my own practice as a manager. I had two role models during the project. The headmaster was a paternalistic autocrat; he did what he felt was right. He expressed his views forcibly and was so consistent that his responses could be accurately predicted. He believed it was his job to lead and to make decisions, although he did use a deputy most effectively to aid decision making. He felt school organisation and management was his sole responsibility. The teacher's job was to teach, preferably quietly and in an orderly manner within the four walls of his or her classroom. The headmistress is a self-professed egalitarian. She favours joint decision making and team building. Her relaxed style borders on a 'laissez-faire' attitude which induces a certain apprehension in the other teachers. However, she is sometimes inconsistent and retreats into a contradictory dictatorial style. I fear I share this inconsistency, which perhaps is a sign of insecurity.

The problem with my style of management is that I am too keen to carry everyone with me, to win over the world. I care too much what others think or feel. I can lose sight of my goals and fall easy prey to the 'games people play', the time wasting, prevaricating and deliberate opposition and aggression from those who basically do not want to change. I hope I have changed somewhat during the course of this project and wish to put forward two forms of evidence for this change. The first is perhaps the more spurious. I wish to refer to Karl Popper's ideas on the intellectual functions of writing, and claim that writing can become an integral part of the thought processes, crystallising, organising and developing ideas. As Popper (1976) says; 'I often find myself mistaken in the belief that "I have got it", that I have grasped a thought clearly; when trying to write it down I may find that I have not got it yet.' So my research diary served another purpose. I would not have analysed, dissected, fretted over happenings, conversations and chance remarks had I not been involved in this action research project. This very analysis has caused me to examine, criticise and change my management style; it has led me to alter rather idealistic beliefs. My experience is limited to two schools. In my previous school I was promoted 'through the ranks', and always had the support and encouragement of my colleagues. My present school has made me grow up, to be prepared for the unexpected, to be tough enough to deal with it and when the occasion demands it, to impose my will on others.

The second form of evidence for change in my practice comes from two questionnaires which I have completed during the course of the project. From my analysis of the first questionnaire I drew the following conclusions: the desire to placate others in the hope of creating a pleasant working atmosphere is perhaps too strong; it would therefore be beneficial to develop a greater awareness and understanding of the total needs of the school. On examining the second questionnaire I find I am much more ready to assume responsibility and give clear directives. I like the concept of a maturity scale; new members of staff require positive direction but as they mature and become more skilful in their jobs they require less and less support. A manager's role therefore is to promote the growth and development of others and to be aware of their level of maturity.

I cannot claim to have changed completely. I do not believe one can adopt a style of management at will. Neither do I believe managers are entirely free to develop their own style; they are constrained by the expectations of those they manage. I am still basically 'people-centred' but I do know more about my own style (my *actual* behaviour, not attitudes, thanks to my research diary) and I am far more aware of the effects of styles of management on others. This knowledge and understanding I am sure can only help me to improve my own practice. I aspire to becoming one of Jennifer Nias' positive leaders who 'set teachers a high professional standard, adopted a dynamic but consultative policy towards decision-making and actively supported the professional development of individuals' (Nias, 1980).

7 The development of co-operative teaching in a semi-open plan infant school

MARGARET FOLLOWS

Co-operative teaching in its context

Much has been written about the increasing emphasis that has been placed on the individual development of children in the primary school and about the responsibility of the class teacher to identify the academic, emotional, social and physical needs of the children, and initiate activities which satisfy these needs. Varying needs have been highlighted, and it is the realisation of this which has moved teachers away from *blanket teaching* to emphasise individual and small group teaching. At the same time there has been a growing tendency to encourage independent and self-directed work by children, with them following an investigative/collaborative approach to learning.

When planning a learning activity for children, the class teacher needs to consider a range of factors. They include:

a. the teacher's aims for the child in the particular curriculum area;

b. when the activity should take place;

c. where the activity should take place;

d. the approach to the activity;

e. why the activity is chosen;

f. with whom the activity is pursued;

g. the materials required for the activity.

To deal effectively with these factors the teacher has to have considerable professional skill and a deep understanding of any particular child's needs. She has to be flexible and imaginative and have the ability to change her approach and use a variety of activities. It is obvious that this requires not only a considerable resource of knowledge and skill, but flexibility in grouping pupils, arranging timetables and using space and resources. The question arises as to whether any one teacher working independently in her own classroom is able to meet this challenge. Advocates of co-operative teaching would say that she is able to do this with efficiency only when she is involved in a co-operative teaching situation. It is argued that by bringing teachers into co-operation, all sorts of benefits are gained.

The Case Study

My case study describes an action management project which resulted in the establishment of co-operative teaching within a three-unit teaching area in a semi-open plan infants school. I would like to use Forward's definition of team teaching to describe what I mean by co-operative teaching. This is 'the joint planning, joint implementation, joint evaluation of some educational activity for a defined group of children by two or more teachers' (Forward, 1971).

The case study school is located in an outer London borough; the catchment area is typical of other urban areas. There is dense housing around the school. The children have a variety of backgrounds, and 50% are from ethnic minorities with many having English as a second language. The school has three teaching areas, colour coded red, yellow and blue. This study focuses on the red area with its 76 children and three teachers. Each teacher is responsible for a class unit. The class units are vertically grouped, with classes R and I containing 6- to 7-year-olds and class A 5- to 6-year-olds.

At the start of the project the situation contained a number of factors, not all conducive to the development of a co-operative teaching situation. To make a success of co-operative teaching in the red area we needed a broad balance of special skills and knowledge. In this we were fortunate as we were all experienced infant teachers and each of us was responsible for one of the three curriculum areas of language, mathematics and multi-cultural education. We were also fortunate in having the clear support of the headteacher.

We were less fortunate in the short-term organisation of teaching within the red area. We had not worked closely together before. My colleague responsible for the third class unit had replaced a temporary teacher, and her priority at the time the project started was to stabilise her position as a new class teacher. An added problem was the fact that I was deputy headteacher and my wider school responsibilities could have interfered with my intention to work as an equal member of a team.

Reconnaissance

This report of my attempt to bring about co-operative teaching in the red teaching area covers the work of two terms. The first term was a reconnaissance time. At the start of the project I was very aware that we all needed time to establish ourselves in the new teaching situation. We needed to assess both our professional/personal compatability and our methods of organising the red teaching area. My dissatisfaction with existing arrangements was shared by the two collaborating teachers. We all expressed concern about the limited teaching space, the unacceptable furniture arrangements, the inaccessibility of the resources to all the children in the three class units and the limited time available for us to meet and plan change. At this point my collaborators did not share my specific concern about the lack of co-operative teaching.

Initially co-operation developed to improve the situation for the benefit of our independent teaching with our own class units, rather than as co-operation to plan flexible groupings of children or the joint use of resources by children in the three class units. It is clear from our informal discussions at the beginning of the project (carefully recorded in my research diary) that what predominated was largely independent self-analysis of our own individual classroom practices.

An important factor in the initial stages of the project was the hierarchical structure of relationship that was established between the three teachers. Our group was not an ideal horizontal structure that could easily undertake the joint elements of decision making involved in joint planning, joint implementation and joint evaluation — all important aspects of action research. I was quite clear that I wanted there to be equal participation in the project. This was the nature of the action research approach that I was using. I wanted to be treated on equal terms, as a class teacher, collaborating within a group of three class teachers, but I felt that the teachers were expecting leadership, in a similar way to the leadership they experienced from me as deputy headteacher. They wanted me to make decisions and resolve difficulties about the project in the same way that I was providing leadership in response to LEA requirements for testing children in mathematics and English.

Questions recorded in my diary show my attempts to understand this problem, a situation that I had not anticipated. The fact that I was deputy headteacher as well as a class teacher was only one of several possible explanations, and in attempting to resolve the difficulties I considered a number of alternative explanations. Was it because I had initiated the project and therefore was considered the natural leader? Was I being too dominant within the group, my wish to succeed preventing the others from becoming full participants? Were the other teachers really concerned about practices in the red teaching area or was their collaboration a political expedient? Were the teachers' reactions reflecting the climate of the school at the time? There were general insecurities related to unstable staffing. Did my collaborators genuinely misunderstand my intentions? Were my intentions clear? Was I being too impatient and expecting things to move too fast? Was I trying to establish a form of teaching that I had experienced previously and they had not?

The development of greater communication and a change in the nature of our collaboration to co-operation as equal participants began with the joint planning of a school journey that involved children from the three class units. This provided the opportunity for planning a common experience for the three classes and for carrying out joint follow-up work. During this time I took photographs of children in the red teaching area and asked the other teachers to help me evaluate what was happening. The photographic evidence highlighted our joint concerns about the arrangement of furniture, the location of resources and their use.

At this stage in the project I felt confident enough to show my collaborators a video recording that I had made in the red teaching area. The video recording showed a new approach I was making with a resource, for my class unit. Groups of children used the television/video recorder independently as and when appropriate to their learning. The recording showed my practice in the classroom; the two teachers were able to help me evaluate what was happening in the classroom. They also decided to introduce a similar use of television/video with their own children and for this we decided to mix children from the three classes as my children were already familiar with the approach. *We had started to plan changes.*

The action

I made use of the action research cycle of planning, action and reflection to move the project forward. I had kept a learning log or diary to monitor the project through the reconnaissance stage and this became increasingly important as the project continued. I would pause to take stock and formulate questions in my diary that would enable me to move forward.

For the duration of the project I was supported by my headteacher, with whom I had regular meetings. In the second half of the project she provided the flexibility of staffing that made it possible for the two collaborating teachers and myself to meet formally once a fortnight during school time to evaluate our action and make further plans.

By the second term my goals of co-operative teaching and flexible teaching groups seemed nearer. We had established agreement on the principle of co-operative teaching with flexible teaching groups, but we needed to ensure that this principle would operate effectively. My collaborators agreed that I should devise a checklist for observing the activity of children from the three class units in the red teaching area. This teaching area, which is a resource area shared by the three class units, contained a number of activities for children. The checklist that we devised included the following activities: wet sand; dry sand; home corner; water; outdoor play area; book activity; shared activity and interest table. We would hold weekly meetings to review the results of monitoring children's activity and to plan changes to facilitate more flexible groupings of children for all three class units. The focus of the observational study was deliberately child-centred as I felt that it was only through the observation of the children's activities that the effects of co-operative teaching could be perceived and enhanced. I hoped that monitoring the use of the red teaching area would result in (a) greater collaboration between the three teachers; (b) the improved use of space in the red teaching area; (c) the improved use of resources in that area; and (d) the establishment of collaborative learning situations and flexible social situations for children.

The children were observed for a period of five weeks. Each activity was observed twice a day, once in the morning and once in the afternoon. The number of children from each class unit engaged in the activity was recorded on the checklist, the letters R, A and I denoting the class unit. At the end of each week the checklist was analysed and discussed by the teachers who then made plans for the following week. Table 1 summarises the number of activities observed and their use by children from a single class, from two classes and from three classes for each of the five week-long periods. The table shows that over the five-week period there was a decrease in the use of resources by children from one class unit, a variation in the use of resources by children from two class units and an increase in the use of resources by children from three class units.

During the *first week* it was clear that resources were predominantly used by class A who made daily use of them, while classes R and I made haphazard

TABLE 1 *The class unit composition of pupils engaged in observed activities in the red teaching area each week*

	Week				
	1 %	*2* %	*3* %	*4* %	*5* %
From single class	77	31	51	32	37
From two classes	20	64	20	46	25
From three classes	3	4	20	22	37
No. of activities observed	35	45	35	41	51

use. Furthermore, on the majority of occasions each class was using a resource independently. The only resource that was shared by the three classes during the observation times was the home corner, a resource naturally promoting the integration of children in a mixed age/ability group. (Throughout the five-week period there was some integration of the children at the interest table and in the book corner at the beginning and end of the day, but this was outside the times chosen for observation.) At the end of week one we met formally to discuss the results from the checklist monitoring. It was agreed that in that week minimal integration of children took place, with little flexibility of groupings to cater for the varying needs of children. We formulated the following questions:

a. Why was there dominance of the use of resources by class A? Was it to do with (i) the specific needs of those children? or (ii) the location of the resources?

b. Why were the children from classes R and I reluctant to use the resources? Was it to do with (i) accessibility of the resources to these children? or (ii) the attitudes of the children (dependent on previous experience before the start of the project)?

c. How important were our teaching methods and our attitudes to the use of resources as part of the learning programmes that we devised? We were each still allocating times for our children to use the resources.

d. Did the physical space of the red teaching area prohibit children from using it?

e. Would children from classes R and I benefit from greater use of the area and its resources?

f. In which ways would it be best to develop flexible groups, related to the mixed ages in the three classes?

g. How could we encourage the children from the three classes to use the resources?

During the meeting we agreed to change our practice of allocating times for the separate use of resources by the class units. We talked about the necessity of collaborative planning to structure activities in the red teaching area to achieve a developmental programme appropriate for the whole 5 – 7 age band. The teachers from classes R and A also planned a shared activity using constructional apparatus for their classes.

In the *second week* resources were used more frequently by children from all the class units, with less dominance by class A. There was also a marked decrease in the use of resources by groups of children from one class, and an increase in children from two classes sharing a resource. This was partly due to the planned constructional activity mentioned above. There was also a slight increase in the number of observations of children from all three classes sharing the use of a resource. It is interesting to note that this was due to activity in the home corner. No observations were made of integration of children at the activity table or book corner although this continued as before at the start and finish of each day. During our second review we discussed the results of implementing the flexible groupings of children from the two classes and considered the value of the collaboration. For the following week we decided to plan activities jointly for children drawn from all three class units around use of the sand and interest tables.

In the *third week* the checklist showed an increase in the times when the resources were used by children from all three classes although there was also an increase in use by one class. The strategy to integrate children's use of the interest table was successful, with children from two or three classes using it for 20% of the times it was observed in use. At the end of the week we reviewed our successful integration of children around the interest table. We recognised that younger children had greater need for access to some resources like sand and water. We decided to extend the red teaching area by making more frequent use of the outdoor play area for water activities and constructional activities that could be shared by all three class units. We planned another joint activity for classes R and A using constructional apparatus.

By the end of the *fourth week* it was clear that the resources were being used more frequently by children from all three classes, and that class A no longer monopolised resource use as had been the case at the start of the monitoring project. There was a definite decrease in the use of resources by a single class. Because of the constructional activity planned for joint use by classes R and A and a shared book activity for use of classes R and A, there was an increase in the use of resources by children from two classes. There was also a continued integration of the children from the three classes with the interest table. At the weekly discussion we decided that there was evidence that flexible groupings had been established. The jointly planned activities had been very successful. We considered other ways in which we could continue the collaborative work, particularly by extending those activities that had already proved successful. We decided to extend to three classes the book activity that had been developed for two classes.

At the end of the *fifth week* there was evidence of a substantial increase in the shared use of resources by children from the three classes. The planned activities had been extremely successful in facilitating the flexible grouping of children from all three classes. Although the five-week monitoring project was at an end, we decided to continue the joint planning of activities and made plans for the relocation of some of the resources to make shared use more effective still.

Conclusion

Action research is about improving one's own practice, one's understanding of the practice and the contexts in which this practice occurs. I would claim to have succeeded in all three of these designs. I have developed my skills, both as a project manager and as a collaborating class teacher within a group of three, and I have brought about improvement in the quality of education both within the classroom and in the school as a whole.

Between my roles as an action research project leader and a deputy headteacher I still feel some continuing conflict. In action research success depends on the commitment of participants, the commitment demanded being over and above what is normally expected of teachers. In most schools this is not supported by the allocation of extra resources such as time, and depends on good will. As a deputy head it is difficult to ask teachers for good will when present debates over conditions of service continue. At my school the situation promises to be better. As a staff we have decided to establish co-operative teaching throughout the school. Time has been made available during regular staff meetings for the essential planning, implementation and evaluation of work.

The results of developing co-operative teaching in the red teaching area have been impressive, both for the teachers and pupils concerned there, and for the school as a whole. The original team of teachers has now separated and each member has become part of a new teaching team of two teachers. The intention is to develop co-operative teaching in these new teams. The project has now become a whole school project, and we plan to monitor the development of co-operative teaching both within each teaching area and between teaching areas, and to evaluate the data collected. The new staffing allocation allows for greater flexibility of staffing and so we plan the integration of the part-time teacher, the English as a Second Language (ESL) teacher and the headteacher into co-operative teaching situations, thus increasing the contact that pupils have with different adults.

For my final point I want to make quite clear my values concerning co-operative teaching. I believe that co-operative teaching promotes flexibility in the organisation of pupil groupings which enables children from different school classes and age groups to work together to their benefit. It enables teachers to share their specialist skills, particularly when they collaborate in planning activities. Children benefit from relating to more than one adult and there is less likelihood that a personality clash between adult and child will produce deadlock. Co-operative teaching enables a broader perspective on the assessment of particular children and on the identification of their needs. Space and resources can be used more effectively. Co-operative teaching also provides a natural induction programme for new teachers. In establishing co-operative teaching throughout a school the action research goal of a critical community of teachers responsible for their own professional development can be achieved. I hope this is the situation we have reached at Follows School.

8 Improving classroom interaction: an action research study

ROD LINTER

The following case study, undertaken in a 12–16 mixed comprehensive school, describes a practising teacher's first experience of action research. Its aim was to improve the quality of classroom interaction in a class of fourth-year sociology students. Its result was to highlight a number of issues that had been hidden before the research was undertaken.

Action Research

I took as my definition of action research that provided by Kemmis & Henry (1984). They emphasise the collaborative nature of action research, essential for the collective professional development of teachers. They define action research as 'a form of self-reflective enquiry undertaken by participants in social (including educational) situations in order to improve the rationality and justice of (a) their own social and educational practices, (b) their understanding of these practices and (c) the situations in which these practices are carried out.' I endeavoured throughout my research to subscribe to the criteria offered by Kemmis & Henry (1984). It was participatory, involving principally myself and 24 fourth-year students. My aim was to consider my own practice and as such I felt that the pupils could offer genuine feedback concerning the educational experiences to which they were being subjected. Towards the end of the study, I found myself asking them to reflect on their practice as learners. Such contributions were collected in the form of questionnaires and interviews. Other information was obtained by means of videotape recordings made in the classroom, whilst audio tape was used as a device to obtain lesson transcripts.

Colleagues were involved, though not essentially to examine their own practice, but rather as contributors of informed opinion and observers of my practice. However, it seemed that self-reflection was an inevitable consequence of being involved even in a supportive capacity. Most of the input from colleagues took the form of conversations which I logged in my research diary, but two colleagues did play a major role. The first acted as a non-participant observer to my classroom practice and later helped in the analysis of videotaped material subjected to analysis by the Flanders (1970) interaction analysis method. She also offered me the facility of observing her in her lessons. This I did to determine if pupils' patterns of behaviour were consistent with those I had noted in my own lessons. My second collaborator was the school's youth tutor — an experienced teacher, particularly in the development of social skills through group work. By taking a lesson promoting the logic of co-operative learning I was offered the opportunity to view my own students, as a non-participant observer, working both individually and in groups for well over an hour in one of his lessons.

Data were thus recorded in a variety of forms: personal observations in a daily log; pupil responses through questionnaires; videos of my own classroom; and written observations I made of my pupils in other classrooms. I also used a sociometric technique which provided valuable insights into the pupils' groupings, highlighting feelings of warmth, indifference and rejection. Such an exercise revealed much about the attitudes of the pupils, the classroom climate and the effective working of groups.

In collecting such a variety of data I followed the grounded theory notion of Glaser & Strauss (1967), i.e. theoretical considerations obtained in data gathered from and applicable to specific social situations which must be studied 'without any preconceived theory . . .' I began with no fixed problem or 'instance', mindful of the premise of Kemmis & McTaggart (1981), that 'one does not need a problem, all you need is a general idea that something might be improved'. A reading of Brophy & Good (1984) had sparked my interest in classroom interaction as a feature of classroom management, an area about which we obtain little feedback. It seemed a valuable and relevant point at which to begin. Such an analysis of my teaching style offered the opportunity to establish that I practised what I preached. Was I living out my educational values? Or was I Whitehead's 'living contradiction' (1980a), or guilty of Ebbutt's (1983) notion of 'performance gap'? Indeed, what was my philosophical standpoint? It was with this 'personalised' question that I began my study. However, the reflective process soon led me to a consideration of issues on a much wider scale. To this end I can briefly summarise my action research into five cycles, each an outcome of the previous enquiry.

1. 'The Reconnaissance Phase': In this phase I set out to examine the values which I sought to put into practice, i.e. to establish a philosophy of practice.

2. 'Lesson Observation and Analysis': Two 30-minute lesson observations were conducted, the data being subjected to Flanders' interaction analysis chart (FIAC). These lessons were also recorded on videotape. The imbalance of interaction with pupils prompted —

3. 'The Question of Bias': Did I favour certain pupils? I considered this by means of a self-perception exercise. This in turn promoted an action plan to increase classroom interaction and to move me towards a style of teaching closer to the values to which I subscribed in cycle 1.

4. 'A Review of Practice': This followed a four-week action plan. Two further lessons were observed and video-recorded and subjected to FIAC analysis to note any change in my practice — the results being compared with those of cycle 2. But what did the pupils think?

5. 'Pupil Feedback': By means of two differing questionnaires and video/audio interviews, I obtained feedback on my own practice. I then sought to get pupils to consider their own practice through self-evaluation of video material. A further questionnaire enquired into their ability to work co-operatively and to contribute to the learning situation.

Discussion

In the first cycle of action research I established my philosophy of practice, and explored the characteristics of my practice utilising Kelly's Repertory Grid (1955). This provides a means to evaluate and develop a perception of practice through a consideration of one's 'personal constructs', which in turn are the product of experience. Kelly proposed that we make sense of our world by comparing things; i.e. we learn to recognise through a process of 'construing' or interpreting from bipolar concepts. Such is the nature of the repertory grid.

An examination of my own constructs revealed some of the values underlying my practice. It revealed that by creating greater opportunity for teacher/pupil and pupil/pupil interaction, in an informal situation, learning would be enhanced. For my part I should avoid teacher domination of lessons and develop areas of pupil interest. I should advocate co-operative learning as a basis for increased classroom interaction but also as a means of developing social attributes and fostering the notion that they (the pupils) are as responsible for their learning as I am. Such participation should involve tolerance and consideration of others.

Two key values to emerge were the importance of pupils' involvement and the importance of their active participation. Certainly these are not revolutionary ideas. Illich (1971) has argued that most learning is not the result of instruction, but rather 'the result of unhampered participation in a meaningful situation'; whilst Hargreaves (1982) has suggested that the involved learner does not seek 'outside approval' if offered a 'balance between individual work and work which involves interaction with peers', particularly where the latter gives opportunity for the pupils to make 'their own contribution in a variety of intellectual and practical responses'. My immediate concern was to assess whether I applied these principles to my practice. Did I, for instance, offer ample scope for speech and for discussion? Did I encourage such a participatory environment? This was the first question I set out to answer.

In the second cycle of action research I analysed classroom interaction by using the Flanders interaction analysis chart (FIAC). This categorises teacher/ pupil verbal interaction within a lesson, every three seconds. However, such a process proved too difficult for my classroom observer — it is an exercise that needs a good deal of practice. As a consequence the FIAC analysis was jointly conducted by myself and the observer using the 30-minute video material of that same lesson. Even then we found three seconds too short a time lapse in which to record data. We therefore settled for a 10-second analysis, mindful of its potential inaccuracies, hoping to redress the situation with further practice. But it did provide a means of data collection, the basis for action.

The reflective process proved 'an enlightening experience — almost worrying', as recorded in my log. I was clearly more aware of the term 'living contradiction'; indeed, it applied to me! By categorising interaction into teacher- and pupil-initiated verbal responses, the exercise illustrated a high concentration of teacher domination. Whilst I realised why this had occurred, I questioned if the experience was rewarding for the pupils. The limited interaction appeared in question/answer periods during which I demonstrated the 'certainty principle', i.e. I required correct answers to closed questions. This was despite the fact that in the previous year an HMI inspection of the school had reported: '. . . most of the oral work is in the form of question/ answer between teacher and pupil. Questions mainly require factual recall and produce short answers . . . pupils are willing to respond but are rarely given the opportunity to extend their answers.' I would not have expected myself to be still guilty in this practice. I also found that my questions were too difficult and that I used terms which were too complex. The analysis revealed a high level of teacher direction and limited opportunity for pupils to express their ideas; rather, a passive acceptance. However, when given the opportunity to work in groups, the video playback revealed them as capable of a good level of participation and as reacting positively to the situation.

Without falling into the trap expressed by Flanders (1970), that one must be wary of the generalisation that 'teacher talk is bad and student good', I did feel that my personal philosophy was not in evidence. Equally alarming was the revelation that out of a class of 24 students, 12 had remained silent, nine of them girls! Were they bored? Shy? Or was I guilty of bias? From this point my action plan had a dual edge. I was concerned to establish more active participation within lessons, but I could not ignore the issue of bias (gender or otherwise).

Cycle 3 was concerned with the question of bias. To consider this I conducted a self-perception exercise enquiring into my personal values, attitudes and preferences. I considered four pupils, two for whom I had positive feelings (one boy and one girl) and two for whom I had feelings of indifference (one boy and one girl). I clarified my feelings about their physical appearance, manner, behaviour, attentiveness, classroom involvement and extra-curricular contact. I concluded that I interacted positively with children whom I found involved, committed and with whom I had extra-curricular contact. My indifference was unconsciously directed at those pupils who took a passive role. Clearly, it seemed this was an uncomfortable and unprofessional state of affairs. I determined to manage a more active role for my pupils, to increase opportunities for teacher/pupil and pupil/pupil interaction and to increase participation by all. In this way I hoped to confront the issue of bias and involvement at the same time, since the two had become inseparable.

a. a decline in teacher dominance within the classroom;

b. greater opportunity for pupil participation;

c. increased opportunities for interation in an informal setting, which would generate a better rapport within the classroom which in turn would actively work against the possibility of bias.

These I sought to achieve through a more student-centred approach where pupils were encouraged to take responsibility for their own learning and to evaluate their own performance and mine. I determined to make greater use of the standard principles of group work within active learning, e.g. to make use of the circle as a means of communication; to break away from the more formal structures observed in the video material; to facilitate better eye contact; and to promote 'listening as a skill'. Indeed, an initial 'Moon Game' activity established the conditions or 'ground rules' necessary for a profitable learning atmosphere, i.e. to respect and value the opinions of others. With these objectives in mind and after a careful consideration of Brandes & Ginnis' *A Guide to Student Centred Learning* (1984), the plan was implemented. However, I was fully aware that change does not take place overnight and that it might take significantly longer than a few weeks for the students to respond fully, if indeed they would.

Cycle 4 of the action research involved me in a sociometric study to compare my feelings with those of the pupils. To monitor any change, two further lessons were videotaped and subjected to FIAC analysis. The relevant trends concerning practice were then plotted on a graph. Other impressions were gained through observation of video material and informal conversations with colleagues and pupils (recorded in my research diary).

Hard and fast conclusions from this part of the study would be premature. But there were indications of change in practice within the classroom, particularly with regard to interaction. There was a movement away from teacher domination and student input increased, both in response to teacher-initiated interaction and to group work strategies. On a personal note, I felt that pupils had developed a greater ease with group work, that the classroom climate had improved and there were more instances of humour, a valuable asset in any learning situation. However, I was aware that these were only impressions and as such highly subjective. The movement away from teacher direction was not complete, but this did not worry me unduly since at times I found myself taking considerable time explaining procedures. Indeed, Brandes & Ginnis (1984) advise the need for such skills to develop in a 'structured situation'.

An analysis of classroom interaction also revealed pleasing changes from earlier observations. It revealed a substantial increase in pupil responses, many of them requiring expressions of values and opinion. I had improved in my capacity to develop and build on pupils' ideas. There were instances of involvement from pupils who previously had not been prepared to contribute in question/answer situations. For example, a transcript of the first lesson subjected to FIAC after the action plan revealed the following dialogue:

RL responds to Cheryl (who had not previously participated), whose hand had been up for a short while.

RL: Cheryl, what were you going to say?

Cheryl: The cadets . . . they all joined the cadets.

RL: What did you think about that?

Cheryl: It was sad . . . and far too strict.

RL: So why do you think schools like these continue with such activities? . . .

Despite the general improvement in question and answer practice, the underlying trend was still one of boys' dominance. Over the three sessions recorded on videotape, only two boys failed to respond, one having a long history of withdrawal noted by the school psychological service, the other having a speech impediment; whereas the corresponding figure for girls not responding was seven, i.e. 50% of the female population — this despite efforts to favour and encourage the girls to respond. I found my enquiry supporting the theme of boys dominating the classroom. This was further fuelled by conversations with other staff recorded in my diary. It reflected the reticence of girls as noted by Stanworth (1981) and the domination by boys of classroom and teacher attention noted by Spender (1978). Such 'reticent' girls could talk quite comfortably with their peers during group activities, but this was not reflected in classroom discussions. Indeed, it would probably be naive to expect that it would, such issues having deeply rooted cultural causes. Yet I did note encouraging signs; one particular diary entry observed: 'Excellent response from all students . . . even managed significant contribution from Laura, Clare, Samantha and Michelle . . . I actively asked them to respond during the "round"; if they did not answer promptly I returned to them later. This practice worked well and is worthy of greater use in the future.'

Cycle 5 of the action research focused on the use of my pupils as collaborators. I was anxious to use my students as 'collaborators', to seek their opinions on both my performance and the lessons to which they were subjected. A general discussion about teaching styles emerged naturally during a sociological debate concerning the relative merits of state and public school education. The following extracts, obtained from videotape material of the third and final lesson analysed by FIAC, reflect the pupils' traditional expectations of the teacher's role but also an appreciation of discussion and collaborative work.

'The teacher should be at the front of the room and after he or she has said what they have to say the pupils should discuss it . . . everybody should have a chance to express their views.' (Lisa.)

'I think the teacher should be at the front and he or she should give out the work and children get into groups, discuss it and write it out themselves.' (Nilesh.)

In response to my question 'But do we really learn anything when we just talk in groups?' the following response was obtained, which illustrated the value placed on 'learning conversations' and collaborative working situations:

'Well, if you're just writing things down your work is not interesting, but if you're talking you pay more attention . . . because you're listening to what others say and you pick things up from them.' (Liz.)

The feeling that group work was enjoyable and promoted participation was supported by the results of an enquiry questionnaire which I asked the students to complete. A complete breakdown of the results here is impossible but it did provide me with some positive feedback concerning my own practice, in that the pupils felt they were learning, understanding, progressing and co-operating. In an open response to the question 'What did you particularly enjoy about the work this term?', 13 of the 22 returns noted group work. The returns also rekindled the issue of gender, in that a considerable number of girls' responses suggested that boys were unable to work sensibly in groups. I thus planned to consider these issues in my next action phase.

To this end I organised random groups and asked the pupils to comment on the effectiveness of the group, e.g.:

'Did you enjoy the experience?'

'Did anyone dominate the group?'

'Estimate your own contribution . . .?'

'What was the group's percentage time on task?'

I also asked them to watch video material of themselves 'in action' to evaluate their own participation and that of others; to try to establish in their own minds the responsibility they had for their own learning; i.e. to reflect on their own practice.

This exercise indicated that whilst the work in groups was enjoyable, the productivity varied enormously, although all pupils felt they contributed well. Again many girls found it very difficult to work in their mixed groups: 'the boys were disgusting' was one extreme comment, whilst those girls working in single-sex groups attributed a high level of 'productivity' 'because there were no boys'. It seemed clear to me that in view of such evidence, we as a staff needed to ensure good practice particularly in the lower school, regarding the effective working of groups and in relation to gender issues. The need to establish a school policy seemed long overdue.

My enquiry had thus led me to consider wider curriculum issues, generated by an initial consideration of my own practice. I had felt that I had reached Whitehead's point of 'self validation', i.e. that what I had done was 'relevant and sound' (Lomax, 1986a), but I needed the assurance of others. As Chambers (1983) suggests, 'action research only becomes action research when its findings, descriptions and data are validated by the perceptions other than those of the teacher'. As such the *meta* process, in which the perceptions of one actor in a specific situation are contrasted with those of other actors in the same situation, is a valuable tool in action research. It clearly puts the researcher in the 'hot seat' in that the constructive criticism offered by such a validation group offers a further reflective phase. In my instance, it was a case of needing to express my claims more clearly. I had become embedded too intimately in both the research and the practice and had failed to 'make explicit the contexts in which the questions and answers occur and to examine the processes operating between questions and answers in a systematic way' (Lomax, 1986).

Conclusions

Had I been involved in action research? Or was it simply curiosity, discovery or enquiry? The terminology seemed unimportant. What was important was that a consideration of practice had been the central theme. I had reflected critically and established my own 'praxis', 'to alter practice from within and therefore to develop and share with others an intuitive understanding of that practice' (Lomax, 1986a).

From a starting point as 'living contradiction', I set out to be more informed. I can make no claims for establishing 'grand theory', but rather for a better understanding of my own practice and for a greater knowledge of my pupils. My claims are that through committed action, I increased levels of pupil/pupil and teacher/pupil interaction within the classroom in an effort to promote a livelier, participative atmosphere. I had moved towards a more active perspective which valued language and discussion and purposefully offered pupils opportunities to express their opinions; i.e. I had moved closer to the philosophy to which I subscribed. In the midst of all this I encountered at first hand the issue of gender bias, the difficulties of its eradication and the problems it presented in the working of groups. Clearly, to teach without an awareness of gender or classroom interaction is to risk allowing internalised attitudes to remain unquestioned and ultimately adversely affect classroom relationships. The outcome of the study is that I need to consider active learning throughout the curriculum; to enable all children to operate as individuals and as members of groups; and to allow children the opportunity to take responsibility for their own learning in a situation where communication through language is paramount and where students are less likely to be dominated by what they perceive to be the expectations of the teacher. Such a situation demands collaborative and self-reflective practice from all teachers acting on whole school policies, a notion clearly expressed in the TRIST Paper of National Interest No. 6 (1988):

> In practical terms we need to encourage teachers to tackle the challenges of active learning in the classroom through team activities. Opportunities need to be created to allow groups of teachers to carry out action research as part of their professional development . . . Self criticism is vital and must be encouraged.

In the light of such statements and the increased demand for teachers to appraise and self-evaluate their practice, action research may become an increasingly common practice in schools. From my own experience this is an extremely time-consuming exercise but is very rewarding. It certainly offers relevance to practitioners, enabling them to think more systematically, critically and intelligently about their practice. Such a process can only bring about benefits for the individual teacher, his or her colleagues and the pupils.

Part III:

Supporting the work of teachers

9 An action research approach to course evaluation

PAMELA LOMAX

This is an account of a course evaluation study that has been in progress since 1984. The course takes place in the Faculty of Education at Kingston Polytechnic. It is a two-year in-service programme of management training for teachers which leads to a recognised award. I use the term *course evaluation as action research* to describe the evaluation strategy, which is based on the techniques of action research. In this account my aim is to examine methodological issues and report on the way in which the process of evaluation has brought about changes in the programme of management training.

Formative Course Evaluation and Action Research

Formative course evaluation has been described as a process of scrutiny, judgement and action designed to implement course improvement (Scriven, 1967). Formative evaluation is distinguishable from summative evaluation by the action component. Summative evaluation is an evaluative statement about past practice; formative evaluation is a statement about progress aimed to promote further action towards improved practice as the statement is being made. Because of this assumption about action, formative evaluation relies on the co-operation of participants (teachers, tutors and administrators). Not only do they have the best understanding of their practice (and need to be involved in identifying it), they are the only ones who can ensure that intentions about course improvement are translated into action. Given a commitment to formative evaluation as described above, it is not surprising that the evaluation strategy chosen should be that of action research.

Kemmis (1985b) spells out this emphasis on practice and collaboration in the following definition of action research:

> Action research is a form of self-reflective enquiry undertaken by participants in social (including educational) situations in order to improve the rationality and justice of (a) their own social or educational practices, (b) their understanding of these practices, and (c) the situations in which the practices are carried out. It is most rationally empowering when undertaken by participants collaboratively.

The formative course evaluation process which I have called *evaluation as action research* is adapted from the typical action research cycle described by Whitehead (Whitehead & Lomax, 1987). I use the term 'spiral' rather than 'cycle' because of the qualitative changes that are likely to occur during the process. Cycles consist of inspection, reflection, judgement and action. Each re-run of a cycle begins on the basis of changed course operation. The cycles are repeated at intervals during the programme, spiralling into the next cycle as a result of the recurring evaluative activity.

Some Issues about Course Evaluation as Action Research

I would like to share with the reader some of my beliefs about course evaluation because they underpin the development of the evaluation strategies used on the management programme. The first issue is the *purpose of evaluation*. I believe that course evaluation should be educational, and that it shares with action research the capacity to be both emancipatory and empowering. What I mean is that it has transformative possibilities — it can create a new order — and this can occur both within the providing institution and within the client institution.

It has been argued that this view of evaluation is located within a radical tradition that fuses fact and value (House, 1986). What is meant here is described by Scriven when he argues for evaluation as a paradigm for educational research:

> 1. Evaluation has the purpose of contributing to the facilitation of education. 2. It relegates the search for theoretical understanding to a secondary position by comparison with the search for improvement. 3. Its parameters are determined by practical problems (particularly as seen by practitioners) rather than by standard methodologies (Scriven, 1986: 54–6).

One reason for the lack of clarity about the place of values in evaluation is that the evidence which can be used as part of the process of evaluation can also be used for accountability purposes and to inform decision making about resource allocation. Although all three processes share a need for the proper collection of evidence, they differ in the use to which that evidence is put. Evaluation does not lack *objectivity* because it includes a judgement of the evidence in terms of a goal that has already been identified as worthwhile; or because the evidence points to more effective ways of achieving the goal; or because the nature of the evidence itself has already moved participants nearer to that goal.

A second issue is the *focus of course evaluation*. I believe that the focus of course evaluation should be student learning — both its effectiveness and its relevance. It is a practical focus. This does not mean that I consider students to have a special prerogative with regard to this learning; I think it should form the centre of a discourse in which teacher-learners, course providers and client organisations like schools and local authorities collaborate. For learning to be transformative, to result in change, it needs to be a reflexive activity. It needs to facilitate our skills of seeing ourselves as in a mirror, and being able to criticise what is reflected. The danger of using standard methodologies to achieve such transformations is obvious.

Jack Whitehead (1985c) employs a dialectical method to move his own learning forward. He identifies aspects of his practice where he sees himself as a *living contradiction* and works to negate the *negation* of his values. This action research approach is crucial for a programme that aims to change participants. I am reminded of a teacher who was about to review the teaching of mathematics in his school when he suddenly became conscious that he was denying, in his current relations with his own very difficult pupils, the very values he was about to propose. He set about solving his classroom problem before embarking on the curriculum reform, but I would predict that he will be in a much better position to advise others after this experience.

Incidentally, I do not think the teacher would have been able to identify and act to resolve his problem without the challenge of critical friends, his colleagues on the management programme. In my view the often colliding perspectives of different participants creates its own dialectic. Both the conversation in which they engage and the critically self-reflective activity that is the focus of that conversation, are empowering and transforming. But it should be noted that the evaluand, the thing to be evaluated, is often retrospective. The process of focusing, of homing in on a particular issue or problem, is what constitutes learning. What is learned becomes clear after it has happened. There is a lesson in this: it may not be useful (or possible) for outsiders to set the agenda for an evaluation.

This raises a third issue, that of *who evaluates*? Kemmis (1986: 118) makes the point that 'the truths to be told about educational programmes are social truths. They are negotiated . . . claims about the programmes are defended and challenged in a process of criticial debate or conversation.' How to harness this debate and conversation, improve its quality and incentive as an activator, is the key issue in evaluation. It is an issue that was not properly addressed by the many programme developers and evaluators who saw the programme as a physical object (rather than a socially negotiated construct) and failed to achieve any change (Stake, 1986; 91).

The nature of an educational programme is not easily accessible to a neutral evaluator, and therefore I think that evaluators should share the values of the programmes they are evaluating (Kirkup, 1986: 68–84). They should not be neutral. This does not mean that the basis upon which they make their judgements cannot be criticised, and accountability has a role to play in this. It is the same for action research. The action researcher investigates her own practice; she can be criticised for doing this badly, but no one else can do it.

I would go as far as to say that evaluation is a meaningful term only when applied by people who are making decisions and judgements about their own practices, and applied to those decisions and judgements. However, the clever evaluator does not keep his head in the ground; holding up a mirror to oneself and one's practices requires the skills of a juggler if done alone. And practice is not only a personal action; it is a set of values that have been handed down and are shared. Programme evaluation must be shared because programmes are shared realities. All the participants have a stake in the programme, whether they are programme leaders, other tutors or students. I believe that this is its strength. It is the lack of neutrality which removes the discordance between knowing and acting that has always been a feature (and a failure) of summative evaluation. Co-evaluation removes the dichotomy between evaluator and client. Those served in the evaluation become those who engage in evaluation. In the spirit of action research they act collaboratively 'to improve . . . their own educational practices, their understandings of these practices and the situations in which they practice' (Carr & Kemmis, 1986).

Course evaluation as action research also mobilises the advantages of asking questions over giving answers (Gadamer, 1975; Collingwood, 1978). Enabling participants to generate the questions in an evaluation maximises the potential for their learning and acting. Such questions focus the evaluation on their concerns and practices, defining the parameters of the evaluation, and generating the critical debate through which better practice is achieved. At its most constructive this form of co-operative enquiry can lead to theory being built through group activity and based on group practice (Kirkup, 1986: 71).

A final issue is *how is the evaluation done?* Kemmis (1986: 118) argues that evaluation involves 'harnessing and refining the ubiquitous processes of individual and public judgement, not in resolving or replacing them with a technology of judgement'. For this reason I have argued that the parameters of an evaluation should not be defined by standard methodologies. But within these parameters there is a place for standard methodologies. A great deal of work has been done on devising strategies that allow people to represent their views without being unduly influenced by others (Lomax & McLeman, 1984). Other strategies exist for quickly documenting information and events and keeping records. Many of these techniques are established favourites within traditional (and quantitative) research designs. As long as the evaluation is a collaborative venture, in which all participants agree about the methodology to be employed, there is no reason why tried and tested procedures should not be used. One of the advantages of course evaluation as action research is that these strategies become the focus for critical debate and action towards improvement alongside everything else in the programme.

The Case Study

This two-year programme of school management training, leading to a recognised award, had its first intake of teachers in January 1984 and evaluation data have been collected from that time. For the sake of clarity I intend to use the term 'programme' to describe the particular course of management training, the term 'teacher' to refer to the participants in the programme and the term 'tutor' to refer to the course teaching team. Three cohorts of teachers have completed the programme; 10 in 1985, 14 in 1986 and 16 in 1988. The 1987 intake (24 teachers) are currently half-way through the programme and a new intake (17 teachers) have just started.

The intention of the programme is to make teachers better at managing schools and parts of school; trouble is taken at the preliminary interview to establish that learning to be better at managing schools involves personal change. On the other hand, the programme itself is conceived as a collaborative learning experience in which tutors as well as teachers are committed to improving their own practice. It is a programme in which teacher participants share with programme directors control over the operation, development and evaluation of the programme. The *purpose of evaluating* the management programme is to improve it so that it becomes progressively better at helping the teachers who participate to become better, in turn, at managing their schools. The reason for monitoring the evaluation is to clarify and confirm how this is achieved so that the methods may be improved and applied elsewhere.

The *focus* of the evaluation can be identified in two main arenas. The first is that of the providing institution; in this arena the question to be answered is how we know that the course is effective and relevant. The second arena is that of the client organisation, the school; here, the question is about how we know that the teacher-manager has improved his/her practice. Both these arenas have implications at two levels. At the micro level, these concern the development of the programme and its clients; at the macro level they concern development of the institutions in which programmes and clients operate. In this account I intend to limit my discussion to the micro issues.

Mechanisms of Course Evaluation

The evaluation of the management programme incorporates three inter-related but separate mechanisms. Review is the relationship between formal provision and the teachers' learning; appraisal is the relationship between the teachers' learning and their management practice; and assessment is the relationship between the teachers' learning/practice and course goals.

The review mechanism

I use the term 'review' when I talk about the way in which teachers and tutors work together to monitor and develop the programme. The review mechanism works through an agenda-setting technique that I have described elsewhere (Lomax, 1985). In its ideal form (as opposed to practice) it should operate in six stages, taking about two hours from stage 1 to the end of stage 4.

In stage 1 teachers are asked to raise issues about the course individually, a tactic to ensure that group pressures do not distort the initial representativeness of items. In stage 2 teachers work in small groups to clarify and reorganise their individual lists; these groups are formed along the lines of pupil age specialisation, as the teachers come from all sectors of education. In stage 3 the teachers work as a whole group to finalise an agenda for discussion with tutors. At the same time tutors meet to prepare an agenda to discuss with teachers. In stage 4 tutors and teachers come together to discuss both agendas and to plan any action that needs to be taken as a result of the discussion. After the meeting representatives of both groups produce a report to be formally tabled at the Course Committee meeting (stage 5). This is an important stage, because it is at this point that deliberations which have been internal to course participants are made public within the more formal monitoring machinery of the Faculty and Polytechnic (stage 6). It is at this level of the review procedure that decisions taken by course participants can be challenged, supported and monitored by personnel and standards which are external to the programme. This has obviously important implications for validating the review mechanism and the action taken as a result of its operation.

The review mechanism is the most institutionalised part of the evaluation procedures. It has existed since the start of the course and has functioned once a term for every group of teachers who have participated in the programme. Part of its success is due to the careful briefing that teachers and new tutors are given early in the programme, and to the fact that it is timetabled and that all tutors (including part-time tutors) are timetabled to attend.

The review has never operated absolutely to plan. In the early stages of a particular programme teachers have made their individual lists, but as soon as working groups have been established they have preferred to work in teams from the start (thus missing out stage 1). Teachers have never completed stage 3 of this process, so that the stage 4 discussion between teachers and tutors has usually worked from several agendas. Despite these modifications, the review procedure has been very successful in keeping tutors and teachers abreast of each others' views on issues concerning the programme. Teachers have been very successful in modifying the programme, making it truly flexible and responsive.

The appraisal mechanism

I use the term 'appraisal' when I talk about the ways in which individual teachers evaluate the effect that participating in the programme has had on their management practice. There are four ways in which this is encouraged to happen.

1. The key to appraisal within the programme evaluation is self-evaluation, which begins in the pre-course period and at the interview when teachers are asked to form plans for their own management development. For the first two cohorts of teachers these personal plans were updated at several points through the programme and also used as a basis for peer appraisal work. This practice has been discontinued in favour of using specific self-evaluation materials that home in specifically on the management activity that the group is addressing at the time. Some of these self-evaluation data have been used by teachers to chart changes in their management approach through the two years of the programme (a case in point is the leadership questionnaire that Kate Burton refers to in her contribution to this volume).

Another important strategy for appraisal is the learning log that teachers are expected to keep from early in the course. Little is known about the success of this activity in the first phase of the course, largely because the activity is not drawn by tutors into the main stream of discussion. I need to investigate this particular issue. In phase 2 there have been some very good examples of teachers using the learning log as a data bank from which to illustrate the dynamics of their group work (they have to write an assessed report on this), and in phase 3 it has been appropriated as one of the main supports for the school-based management project. Teachers' learning logs are not public documents and what is written in them is shared only with the tutor or the peer group at the choice of the teacher. Those teachers who have made information from their logs public suggest that through the log teachers are able to build up their analytical and evaluative skills. For the most successful the log changes from a source of useful quotes to a powerful tool for the documentation and analysis of action research cycles.

At the end of the programme I ask teachers to provide accounts of their perceptions of their development over the two-year period, and to document job changes. These data triangulate with other data to give me a more rounded view of the programme. In fact the job mobility of teachers has increased since 1984, and few teachers in the last cohort to finish the programme were in the same post they filled at the start of the programme. I will discuss the implications of this for the relationship of the programme and the client institutions later.

2. The second aspect of the appraisal mechanism is peer appraisal. There are induction activities in the first part of the course which enhance team skills and facilitate the teachers' work in small groups in phase 2. More formal peer appraisal work within and between teacher cohorts has been tried but has not been successful, as has clearly emerged at review time. For phase 2, teachers work in small teams within which they are encouraged to support each other in relation to school pressures as well as to work together on tasks set within the course. From the inception of the management programme this part has worked well; groups have become closely knit, intense, people/task oriented groups. For the first two cohorts these groups were disbanded at the end of phase 2 and new groups formed in phase 3 to act as formal support groups. This produced a great outcry from the teachers and for the last two cohorts the groups that form in phase 2 have been retained as support sets in phase 3.

The success of support sets is highlighted within the data from review sessions and supported by an independent study that I carried out last term. Support sets have become essential vehicles for collaborative work, particularly in the last phase of the programme when the teachers are working in the comparative isolation of their own schools. None the less, the study identified areas where the work of support sets could be improved, and many teachers felt that the effectiveness of support sets could have become apparent much earlier if teachers had been aware of their value earlier.

3. The third aspect of appraisal is the tutor/teacher dimension. In the initial years of the course this was formalised and the course leader had taped discussions with each teacher. This time-consuming procedure was seen to be extremely beneficial by the teachers, the records of these conversations being made available to teachers as a starting point for further peer appraisal work with fellow participants. For a later cohort we have tried the practice of allocating a particular tutor to a group of teachers, a tutor who would act as a resource and make him/herself available if required. It remains to be seen how well this has worked. It is important to re-emphasise here that I see the tutor as a *collaborator*, working with teachers to enhance their management practice, rather than as an expert or mentor. There is evidence that this view is shared by teachers on the course and is becoming part of a wider course reputation. None the less, this is an area that is ripe for further investigation.

4. Perhaps the most important aspect of appraisal concerns the role of the participating teachers' professional colleagues in their schools. This is the most difficult aspect of the evaluation scheme as it involves integrating the client institution into the evaluation process. Headteachers of the client schools are viewed as important members of the management programme and their support for the course members is required before the client is accepted. Although it was intended that tutors should visit the headteachers and client institutions, only a few such visits have occurred. A similar intention was to keep headteachers informed of the progress of the course (not of the teacher), but this has happened infrequently and without any positive return. I have also approached headteachers after the completion of the programme, but received little useful feedback.

During phase 3 of the course headteachers play a crucial role, because teachers are engaged in school-based action management projects that are possible only with the support of headteachers. Headteachers have not been kept adequately posted about these projects by college tutors, but there is evidence that many teachers have been successful in engaging the collaboration and help of their heads. In some instances this has been more easily achieved than getting the participation of fellow teachers. The support of headteachers has been particularly visible where teachers have invited headteachers to validate their projects.

Validation meetings have been another great success in the development of the course. These were initiated for the 1986 cohort. A validation meeting is where a group of critical friends meet together to consider the teacher's claims about her project and to judge the appropriateness of the evidence she has to support these claims. Validation meetings are attended by the teacher, a tutor, one or two members of her support set and one or two people from her school. Only one teacher in the last cohort failed to hold a validation meeting, and only one did not persuade a school colleague to attend. Several teachers invited their headteachers, and one headteacher (who was a course participant) invited two members of her staff. After the validation meetings I collected information from all the participants including the visitors from the schools. This has provided corroboration for my view about the success of this type of activity, as well as useful suggestions for making the occasions even more effective.

The assessment mechanism

I use the term 'assessment' to refer to the formal requirements that teachers have to meet in order to be awarded a diploma. The Diploma in Professional Studies in Education (DPSE) is awarded by the Council for National Academic Awards (CNAA). The assessment regulations were originally proposed by the course teaching team and agreed by the CNAA. Although teachers were consulted about the original design of the course (market research) it would be incorrect to say that they influenced the assessment procedures.

In what ways can I claim that assessment is part of the evaluation process and conforms to evaluation as action research criteria? Changing the assessment regulations is a lengthy business and although this can be (and has been) done in response to teacher review, the time length of the programme precludes the benefit of such change accruing to those who have initiated it.

I would like to argue that it has been possible within the regulations to make assessment responsive to the evaluation process. The original assessment pattern remains the three-phase affair based on coursework assessment that was written into the first course document. For the early teacher cohorts (1984 and 1985) assessment was wholly tutor-controlled and based on written assignments. The subject of these written assignments has always been open to negotiation by teachers, but not the assessment. It was the 1985 cohort of students who suggested changes in the way assessment was conducted and who achieved a change in the assessment regulations. This change affected phase 2 assessment and introduced the assessment of group work and verbal presentation. It also introduced self and peer assessment alongside tutor assessment.

At present the formal assessment requirements are as follows:

— Phase 1 assessment (after two terms) requires teachers to submit one assignment chosen from several carried out. The achievement of a satisfactory grade on this allows the teacher to move to phase 2.

— Phase 2 assessment comes in the third and fourth terms. It contains three elements: there is a long report which describes the process and product of a group assignment, a school prospectus and a group presentation.

— Phase 3 assessment is in two parts; it is based on a report written about a school-based project undertaken by the teachers. An interim report is presented during the sixth term of the programme and the final report is presented up to three months later.

Each of these phases of assessment presents different problems in relation to their incorporation into an effective programme evaluation process.

I believe that teachers should be implicated in the assessment of their own work and am working to make the management programme more compatible with this belief. For phase 1 assessment I have tried to implicate teachers by involving them in the following way. I asked the 1987 cohort to grade their own assignments using criteria that I had designed. I monitored the results of this and compared their grading with grading done by tutors. In all but two cases teachers' grades were lower than tutors' grades (one tutor would not take part in this exercise). With subsequent practice the discrepancy between teacher and tutor grades has diminished. For the present cohort, about to submit their first assignment, I have asked them to list their criteria, shown them my criteria and said that I would accept either my criteria or theirs with the work. I await results.

For phase 2 assessment, the report and prospectus lend themselves to joint assessment as described above but I have not put this into operation to date. The assessment of the group presentation was introduced as a result of a teacher review session. The teachers designed the assessment procedure which is based on an amalgam of judgements made by the group making the presentation (self assessment), the other teachers (peer assessment), the tutors and two visiting headteachers. The principle of teachers setting their own criteria is well established now for this part of the course and is working well.

For phase 3, teachers have not been involved in the assessment of their work although the validation process that has been described could be integrated with the assessment of the interim report. I will be exploring the possibility of this for the next round of phase 3.

Methodological Problems

I have argued that course evaluation as action research involves the cyclic activity of inspection, reflection, judgement and action; and that this spirals into further cycles. It is not a neat formula and anyone who has been involved in action research will recognise that many different things are going on at the same time; multi-cycles and spirals. It is clear to me that review, appraisal and assessment, as I have defined them, relate to programme activities that are inter-related and difficult to separate. Action within one cycle might be inspection in terms of another. For example, both the review and appraisal aspects of the process begin at the point where teachers' normal practice and the management programme set up a mutual challenge to the values underpinning both — a reflexive situation in which either side responds through the discipline of the action research cycle; but the result on the one hand is in terms of appraisal and changed management practice, and on the other course review and a changed programme. To clarify and make public such a complex process is difficult, yet such clarification and publication is an essential requirement of action research.

My aim as the course leader of a school management course is to bring about improvement in teachers' management practice. This means reviewing carefully my own practice as a course leader and tutor, and ensuring that the programme is an effective vehicle for teachers' management development. I see course evaluation as a mechanism for increasing the effectiveness of the course and therefore achieving my aims for the course.

Methodologically there is a problem in defining and operationalising a definition of improvement. I have focused on three interfaces in defining improvement: programme provision and teacher learning (review); teacher learning and teacher practice (appraisal); and teacher learning/practice and programme goals (assessment). I see improvement as increasing the relevance of the course; as increasing the effectiveness of teachers as managers, thus ensuring that 'learning' is practised; and increasing the match between course goals and teachers' achievements.

The criteria I use to spell out improvement are refined collaboratively by participants during each evaluation episode and should be viewed in context. This method of determining standards is criticised as subjective by some writers; but I would argue that its validity is confirmed in three ways. First, the standards are negotiated by all course participants, both clients and providers. The tendency is for such negotiation to settle at a level far above the lowest common denominator. Secondly, the negotiation occurs in the two arenas of providing body and client institution, thus representing the academic interests of the educators and the pragmatic interests of the practitioners. Thirdly, the negotiation is conducted by course participants within frameworks that are linked into other institutional procedures. These latter procedures provide what is commonly viewed as 'objective' validation.

Kemmis (1986: 118) claims that 'evaluation is the process of marshalling information and arguments which enable interested individuals and groups to participate in the critical debate about a specific programme'. This raises two methodological issues. How does one induct teachers into the procedures of formative evaluation? As the procedures will be in the hands of participants, participants need to be clear about the role they are playing and willing to engage in it. During the four years in which I have documented this case study, this has been a major priority. I would recommend (a) clarification at the preliminary interview of course participants' responsibilities in relation to course review, personal appraisal and assessment; and (b) a fairly explicit contracting session at the induction meeting. Similar precautions need to be taken with tutors. The role of the headteacher of the client school is also crucial. I have found that although headteachers are willing to sign declarations to say they will support their teachers, unless they are carefully involved in the work it does not happen. A closer working relationship with the heads of client schools is one of my major priorities. In my experience difficulties have emerged because the briefing has been inadequate and participants have been confused about their roles, rather than because they have been unwilling to commit themselves to the process.

The second issue raised by Kemmis' statement relates to teachers' ability to participate in critical debate. The emphasis on self and peer appraisal in the case study is potentially problematic. For most teachers 'practice is largely guided by tacit knowing, by naturalistic generalisation, formed from experiencing, often implicit' (Stake, 1986: 100). Self-appraisal is an unconscious activity that is made public and explicit with great difficulty. Similarly, peer appraisal is hindered by teachers' reluctance to appear critical of each other. Both these important evaluative activities need practice and support if they are to be effective. I think that both these skills have been demonstrably enhanced, this view being backed by evidence about the huge success of the support set and the validation meeting.

The outcomes of teachers' critical debate also need to be recorded. A major part of teachers' concern at recording this sort of data is not knowing what to record. I have found that diaries or learning logs can help both as a method of recording and as a way of enhancing self-evaluative skills. What is clear is that teachers cannot be expected to engage in an evaluation programme which requires complex skills without practice in these skills.

An important feature of the case study was the partial integration of assessment into the evaluation scheme. I am still concerned that there is insufficient corporate responsibility in the scheme as it operates. The participants in the management course are mature, experienced people and it has been suggested that they could be trusted to make reasonable decisions about the assessment of their own work. I hope to move forward in this area and am grateful for the critical support that I have received from John Cowan (which is documented in the next chapter).

The involvement of teachers in their own assessment highlights the important methodological issue of the degree to which 'subjective' evidence can be believed, particularly when the subject has an interest in the outcome. The most difficult of the questions posed earlier in this chapter was to do with determining whether teachers' apparent learning on the course was reflected in their changed practice as managers in school. Evidence about their practice came mainly from self-report; the learning diary; appraisal interviews; their account of the action management project. These were different media through which they accounted for their practice, and the media imposed different constraints and benefits. The diary had the advantage of painting a picture over time; the appraisal interviews provided a consultative framework within which critical questioning by others was a common feature; the long report made demands for analytical skills and evidence. The validation meeting made public the teachers' claims to an audience that was knowledgeable about their work and critically sympathetic to their aims. Was such triangulation sufficient safeguard of the reliability of the evidence about practice?

There were a number of problems in approaching headteachers for information after the programme had ended. In at least 50% of cases for the first intake of teachers, the headteachers in post at the end of the course were not the ones who had undertaken to support their teachers at the start. This was mainly due to the job mobility of the teacher group. One teacher had herself become a headteacher at the end of the course. Of the remaining headteachers, some did not feed back any information about their teachers, partly I suspect for reasons to do with their view of professionalism, partly because they were not sufficiently committed to the enterprise to give up their time. Of the responding headteachers, there were those who confirmed other evidence which suggested that teachers' practice had not been greatly affected by participation on the programme; there were those who contradicted other evidence; and there were those who were extremely supportive of both teacher and course throughout the two years (to the extent that they made some contribution themselves to the course) and who were willing to give considerable feedback. It has become evident that approaching headteachers after the completion of the programme is not a good way of getting feedback. More recently, better feedback has been available in the fact that headteachers have been willing to give up their time to attend validation meetings set up by the teachers.

What did They Learn?

Despite the methodological problems involved in course evaluation as action research I would like to claim the following. As a result of the course review mechanism the course has succeeded in adapting to the changing needs of the teachers. New needs have been generated in part by teachers moving to jobs with greater management responsibilities during the course; but more important, needs have been clarified as teachers have become more competent in their diagnosis of their own and their institutions' practices, and this competence has been facilitated by the appraisal mechanism.

Both Course Committee Minutes and Examination Committee Minutes give evidence of fundamental changes in the management and operation of the course that have resulted from the review mechanism, such as changes that occurred in the assessment of the course. In weighing up what teachers learned from their participation in the termly review sessions (from the evidence of their review agendas) it is striking that they learned to take increased responsibility for the course and for their own success or failure to learn within it. In other words, they learned to apply the skills of self-assessment, critical analysis and evaluation in a constructive rather than a destructive way. No small part of this learning was due to the appraisal mechanism which enabled growing self-awareness and self-evaluation. Evidence from the long taped interviews with the 1984 intake at the end of their course and the post-course questionnaire completed by seven of the 10 teachers substantiated this.

What did they learn? How can I judge whether this in-service programme of training has led to improvement in the management practices of participants? Tutors claim that evidence from formal assessment (monitored by the examination procedures of the institution and checked by the external examiner) demonstrates that learning has taken place. Teachers claim improvements in their own practices which are documented in their various reports. Headteachers and colleagues have supported these claims in formal validation meetings. Each piece of evidence standing alone is not a sufficient picture of improvement and therefore not sufficient basis for judgement about improvement, but triangulated they present quite a formidable account of a teacher's progress or lack of progress over time.

10 Reflecting on the action: questions of assessment and accreditation

PAMELA LOMAX and JOHN COWAN

In this chapter the authors engage in a dialogue which was stimulated by Pamela Lomax's account of course evaluation as action research, reproduced in the previous chapter. This is the incentive for them to reflect critically on their own practices in relation to the assessment of students on award-bearing courses. Their dialogue leads to agreement that assessment, as part of the learning process, should be largely under the control of those being assessed. The account illustrates the way in which critical friends can work together to bring about a better understanding of their own and each other's practices.

John: I hope you would agree that formative appraisal is about the relationship between the students' learning or development and their aspirations, the form of the comparison being in the progress which the students still hope to make. Whereas summative appraisal, which would surely be a part of a course evaluation, would ask me (if I were a student) to compare my learning with the course goals *for me*, and determine the extent to which the deficiency arose because of weaknesses in the course, or to which credit was due to the course because my performance so nearly matched my aspirations. I need to differentiate between looking at a *course* formatively or summatively, and looking at my *learning and development*, as a participant in the course, formatively or summatively. I agree that the two are inter-related; but the latter is only a small part of the former.

Pamela: I think there is a case for focusing on different aspects of what I will call the *educational experience*, particularly to distinguish *the course from students' learning and development*. But I think that the total 'educational experience' is about 'students' learning' and we should therefore define 'the course' in terms of this. I solve this problem for myself by using two terms:

review and appraisal. Both are to do with student learning. I use 'appraisal' when focusing on students' learning in relation to their changing practice (what you call development), and the term 'review' to indicate the relationship between students' learning and course operation.

Let me concentrate for a moment on the aspect of appraisal. By *appraisal*, I mean a process in which the relationship between students' learning and students' practice is examined. I have tended to see appraisal linking students' learning to development of their practice rather than (as you do) to aspiration. I suspect that I include aspiration in my package called *learning* while you include changed practice in your package called *learning*. Perhaps it would be useful to be more explicit about both by seeing appraisal as a process in which students' learning is examined by focusing on the relationship between aspiration and changed practice?

For teachers on the school management course that I talk about in the previous chapter, appraisal involves an introspective examination (self-appraisal) or speculum (peer and tutor appraisal) of what has happened so far on the course and what is to be learned from that in relation to teachers' current practices of management. The operation of appraisal, within the management course, follows the pattern of the action research cycle with its four conditions of inspection, reflection, judgement and action. This cycle leads the students to new understandings of their own practices as teachers and school managers. These new understandings become the starting point for further cycles which spiral out from the original concerns in different ways. It's not a tidy process and students learn to engage more rigorously in the four conditions as the course proceeds and as their evaluative skills are refined.

John: I like the four conditions of inspection, reflection, judgement and action — provided you will go along with the idea that the judgement could be of the nature of the scope for improvement as well as of the final standard of performance.

Pamela: My whole thesis of *course evaluation as action research* depends on the judgement always being of the nature of the scope for improvement. There is no room in my model for final standards of performance, therefore no question of judging them. I cannot conceive of a situation in education with no possibility of improvement — if only because it would be a contradiction of the value position implicit in the word 'education'. I choose to use an action research method because it demands the continual refinement of what we take to be standards. In action research the four conditions of inspection, reflection, judgement and action occur in small evaluation cycles that spiral into other cycles. What you might call the final standard of performance is never reached. We never finish learning. There is no end to the spiral.

John: I think the main point I am trying to bring out is that I find it helpful to make a distinction between two types of judgement — the judgement which leads to action (and is associated with what I am repeatedly calling formative processes) and the judgement which determines a standard and is summative.

Pamela: I would be willing to use the notion of standard in the sense of a temporary marker, where we stop and take stock. The marker could be called summative in the sense that it is based upon what has happened up until then. This summative totting up is integral to a formative process. This is different from the idea that there are absolute standards against which a person's achievements can be summed up and judged. I think that this latter notion of summative evaluation is non-educational. I find it distasteful just because it describes situations where judgements and action are not *necessarily* related. This is where the actions and judgements (interpretations of the actions) are owned by different people who may not share the same value position. Incidentally, although I think that the value blindness of outsiders is a valid reason for being wary about their judgements, I do recognise that the cussedness of insiders may make it doubly difficult for outsiders to appreciate what is going on. I think this issue is dealt with by both Pat Broadhead and Hugh Busher in the final chapters in this collection.

John: Then let's not consider it here. But moving towards agreement on vocabulary, by which I am letting you be like Humpty Dumpty, and choosing to make the words mean what you use them to mean, I sense that defining 'review' is more important to you in your argument than it would be in mine.

Pamela: For me the concept *course evaluation as action research* describes the whole process of developing students, staff and programme. Within this process I distinguish three aspects: appraisal, review and assessment. I have already talked about appraisal and will come back to assessment later. Review is important because it highlights the interface of student/staff evaluation. Review, like appraisal, is a series of spiralling cycles made up of the four conditions. Review facilitates the responsiveness of the programme and the tutors to the needs of the students and their learning. I would argue that an evaluation process that did not include this possibility would be failing to maximise the extent of students' learning.

John: My experience has predominantly been with situations in which either the students and I set up the formal provision together, or I set up a procedural framework within which the contract is decided either jointly or as a response to the declared or perceived needs of the class group, week by week.

Pamela: Does this mean that a review procedure is implicit in the learning situations you set up? I agree that review needs to be built into a teaching programme rather than tacked on to the end. But there are dangers if the review process is not made formal. Leaving course review to the good will of tutors is dangerous because it can be fudged. You seem to be suggesting that you rely solely on your intuitive understanding of the situation for feedback (as most teachers do). I don't think it's good enough even for the perceptive tutor; it certainly will not provide adequate feedback for the tutor who is a marginal performer.

John: The only reason, I suppose, that I have not formalised the review procedure is because it hasn't occurred to me that that might be one of the desirable options. It is not *because* I involve my students from the start of the programme — that just *happens* to be the way I operate. Of course there are dangers in any teaching and learning situation if the educational process is not properly evaluated — preferably from a detached standpoint. I would always do everything in my power to obtain such an evaluation, even if only of fragments of what I am doing. And I would never rely solely on my intuitive understanding of the situation, because I know that this is often wrong.

Pamela: I am not sure that I agree when you say that it is preferable to evaluate from a detached standpoint. I think that an evaluator should *at the very least* share the values of the thing being evaluated. Ideally, evaluation should be a participatory activity. If I was talking about a course I would say that it was a corporate responsibility. But perhaps you mean that evaluative judgements should be based on rigorously collected evidence and that the people involved should be held to account? There I would agree. One of the great successes of the review procedure that I am using was when the students and tutors (as a result of an evaluative activity) corporately developed a new assessment scheme and had it accepted by the course validation authority.

John: I must admit that I was a bit worried about the authority which came out of the assessment mechanism you describe in your paper on the evaluation of the school management course. Your students are mature teachers, much more mature than my undergraduates. Yet they *have to* prepare a written report in which they *have to* demonstrate . . . and this is assessed by tutors!

Pamela: Assessment is the third aspect of the evaluation process I have been describing and I would admit that it has been the most problematic in terms of my thesis of *course evaluation as action research*.

I use the term *assessment* to indicate a process in which the relationship between students' learning and course objectives is examined. Where it is formal assessment the relationship is between *demonstrated* students' learning and *published* course objectives. This is an area of course operation that is highly bureaucratised in my institution and not open to the immediate influence of students and tutors. It involves accountability issues that are partly outside the control of the course.

I recognise that the language I used in the previous chapter (language that was taken from the original validated course submission) is authoritarian. Part of recent course development has been to modify both that language and (I admit) the original assessment philosophy. I think that my discussions with you about assessment have been influential here. Unfortunately, changing assessment regulations (and practice) is a lengthy procedure. The School Management course was validated by CNAA. The award is confirmed by an examination committee acting for CNAA. There is an external examiner accountable to CNAA who must ensure that the course is examined in line with the specifications set out in the validated document. I am sure you are familiar with all this.

John: The Polytechnic of North London managed to satisfy CNAA with a scheme in which students chose their own objectives — within an agreed procedure. I don't see any reason for believing that similar freedom with regard to assessment would not be possible.

Pamela: I am not saying that it is not possible to make assessment more student-controlled, only that we have to change something we ourselves set up originally. As part of that process of change, I have to persuade my own institution to allow students some responsibility for their own assessment. But as I said earlier, changes have been made.

Let me describe the progress made so far with phase 1 assessment. This assessment (after two terms) is based on a report chosen by the students from several they have written. Since 1986 students have graded these reports using my criteria. I have also graded them. Both grades are sent with the sample of work to the external examiner. I would include in the sample any work where there was a great discrepancy between my grading of the work and the students' grading of the work.

I have data for two student cohorts (1986 and 1987) comparing tutor and student grading of phase 1 reports. Initially I was forced to make the criteria I use explicit in order to conduct this experiment (requiring a very careful examination of my own marking practice). With the 1986 intake, I presented the students with the criteria and asked them to grade their reports after the reports had been written. With the 1987 intake I gave the students a copy of the marking scheme before they had written the report. With both cohorts, the students applied the criteria much more harshly than I did but the discrepancy between my grades and the students' grades is greater for the 1986 cohort.

John: I was interested to hear about a colleague's experiment which was carried out with a group of participants somewhat similar to yours. He took the step of giving them final authority on assessments — with impressive results, which included one of the group referring himself in the first module. So, to some extent, I was a little bit uncertain about the joint approach to corporate responsibility which you have described. I know it's possible, because so many people do it. It's just that I either can't do it, or don't believe in it. I find that if responsibility is only shared, the consequence is imprinting or attempts to follow the teacher's lead, declared or otherwise.

What I am getting at is that for me assessment has two components, each of which are of importance. I don't care what we call them; but I want them to be identified separately. If I assess the answer which a student gives to an examination question in a conventional situation, I match that product against my model answer, and I identify the relationship between the student's performance and my objectives or expectations in that answer. Whatever the two items concerned may be in a particular situation, there is an element of *comparison* here — and that is the first concept which I would associate with assessment. If I continue with my assessment to produce a mark, then I need to establish some kind of yardstick or criteria list. My second concept is therefore that of having a yardstick or a benchmark. For me the process of assessment contains both the formulation and the use of the yardstick.

I want to suggest to you that the involvement of the learner in self-assessment will vary depending on whether or not it is the comparing or the defining of the yardstick (or both) which are passed over to the learner. I would argue that learners who are totally responsible for making the comparison and the decisions which emerge as a consequence of that comparison, tend to identify for themselves the inadequacy of their learning, and move towards deeper learning and more meaningful understanding — through awareness. Learners who are engaged in the formulation of criteria and hence in the definition of benchmarks or yardsticks have a commitment to standards which they can never have when these are formulated for them. (Boyd & Cowan, 1985.)

The issue I would like to raise — and perhaps stress quite strongly — is the business of passing over responsibility entirely to the learners. This matters enormously to me; I think it completely changes the character of the event, and of the learners' reactions to it, when they know that whatever happens you will not take back authority and will accept their judgement.

Let me try to formulate my argument in a single sentence — or perhaps in just three: (a) making a judgement on my own is a totally different experience from making a judgement and checking it against the judgement of my teacher; (b) that former experience, if repeated several times, can have a distinctly constructive impact on my learning and development; (c) once I have passed through the phase of being able to take responsibility for my own self-assessment. I will then have become big enough to consider and to discuss the judgements which my teachers make about the same work. But without the experience of standing on my own feet, I will always tend to be dependent and subservient.

Pamela: I am in complete agreement. You are describing the central tenet of action research — the importance of participation. My argument with you is that tutors should also retain their place as participants — their equal share of the action. I would want it to be the case that students' grading had equal (but no greater) status than tutor's grading. Generally the differences that have occurred between student and tutor grades for the two cohorts that I have studied have been disagreements about classes of success. Where work has gone to the external examiner he has sometimes supported the student's grade and sometimes supported the tutor's grade. My dilemma is that I do not think students really believe that their grades are treated as equally valid beside tutor grades.

John: I tend to believe things because I have had experience consistent with that developing belief; and I believe that students do the same. If you want your students to believe that whatever happens you will not take back authority, then you must arrange a succession of experiences for them in which — for some of them — that will be their experience. I would strongly advise anyone against passing the authority for assessment to learners unless they propose to have at least two similar experiences of this kind in succession, within the one course of the module. It has been my experience that students who award themselves outrageous marks seldom do so twice — and never three times in succession. So I believe that this is likely to be the pattern. The advantage of repeated experiences is that students can disperse their suspicion that you will interfere if you disagree.

But I would like to move on to raise the whole question of ownership of criteria. The situation you describe for your phase 1 assessment is the classic one in which *you* own the criteria, even if only partly. But because you are the authority and the experienced one, even if ownership is said to be joint, your participation in it is more important than theirs. The difference between your situation and that of my colleague reported above, as I perceive it, is that his students owned the criteria without his involvement. And, in terms of my earlier comment, they had a commitment to these criteria which they had worked out, not just in terms of vocabulary, but much more importantly in terms of the concepts and standards on which they were based.

Pamela: You have certainly convinced me that students should own the criteria by which their work will be judged and I intend to put this into operation with phase 1 of the 1988 student intake. I see it as integral to a process of corporate responsibility in which student participants (teachers with managerial responsibilities) share with programme directors control over the operation, development and evaluation of the programme.

John: This corporate responsibility is an enormous idea. I was tempted to say that I don't believe that it can work — and then I realised that what I meant was that, in terms of my inadequate attempts in the past, I don't believe *I* can make it work — which is a different point, of course. Naturally the hidden curriculum of assessment is even more important than the declared course objectives in controlling the learning which emerges. And that is why the controlled responsibility for assessment is so critical in determining the nature of the learning in a given programme.

Pamela: Yes. But I try to bring the hidden curriculum of assessment in line with declared course objectives through a global programme of action which enables myself, my colleagues and my students to take corporate responsibility for the whole package of this management training. I am not claiming success but intention. A major problem, as you said earlier, is that students need to be inducted into such responsibility. I do not think that self-assessment aids students' development if it is constrained by externally imposed assessment criteria, teaching programmes and programme objectives. In order to have a real influence on assessment, students need to be involved in setting the criteria (I do agree with you). In order to set effective criteria, they need to be involved in developing the teaching programme and the course objectives. Within the total evaluation package that I am suggesting, students can influence teaching programmes and programme objectives and can (and have) altered the assessment procedure. But this process of course development that I am describing is a slow process and it hasn't gone as far as I want it to go. It can only go as fast as all participants want it to go because it is negotiable and historical, and it is not just *my* ideas that count.

However, the course does include a component in which the assessment conforms more closely to your ideal assessment than that I described for phase 1. Phase 2 assessment (at the end of term four) contains three elements. There is a long report which describes the process and product of a group assignment; a school prospectus; and a group presentation. I want to focus on the last. The assessment of a group presentation came about because of a recommendation by an earlier cohort of students and tutors as a result of the course review process. The assessment procedure was designed by students as a group assignment in 1985. (It would be open to new cohorts of students to suggest changes to this but none has chosen to do so.) An assessment is made on the basis of grading done by the group making the presentation (self-assessment), by other students (peer assessment) and by the tutors and consultant headteachers (tutor assessment). Each student group making the presentation has devised its own criteria for the assessment of presentations since this scheme came into operation in 1986. I have data on this for both the 1986 and 1987 student cohorts.

John: Fools rush in where angels fear to tread! I take the view that there must be a beginning some time — and I invite first-year students, who have never written a formal report on an engineering topic, to devise their own criteria at the same time as they identify their goals. They don't do it very well the first time — or even the second or third time. But this learning is a slow and iterative process, and I have taken the line that the sooner it begins the sooner a satisfactory standard will be achieved.

Pamela: I suspect that there might be real grounds for disagreement between us about assessment because I do believe that teachers have a responsibility to comment upon the *quality* of students' work, and commit themselves to a *judgement* about it. However, I do not think that this comment and judgement should be considered any more seriously than the comments and judgements that students make about their own work. Ideally both comments should be available to an independent judge concerned to moderate between the work of a group of students. Unfortunately few institutions have the resources necessary for the proper validation of judgements, and tutors are given the difficult task of being both effector and selector.

John: Like you, I believe that tutors have a responsibility to comment on the quality of students' work, for if we don't do that, then the concepts of rigour and depth, which are learned only when they are exemplified and experienced, may never be mastered by the learners — because they never encounter them. But if we look at phase 3 of your course, where teachers are based in schools, and it is an account of a management project they have undertaken in school that is assessed, I am much less certain about the responsibility which tutors have to commit themselves to a judgement about teachers' work. First of all, in a situation where the tutor cannot possibly appreciate all the pressures on the managing teacher, only the teacher herself can really know how well she has coped with the problem. Do we honestly believe that these mature adults, shown the issues, encouraged to think through the criteria, and accustomed to making judgements, are not capable of making a mature and balanced judgement about such a *teased out* topic as their performance in phase 3?

Pamela: Phase 3 of the course is difficult to assess because it is school-based. It is the teacher's reflections on an action management project she has conducted in her own school that is assessed. These reflections are presented in a two-part report, the first part containing the planning and methodology and the second part an account of action, the final part being presented after the teacher has finished the course. I would agree that such work should be validated by its owners and their peers, and with the 1987 intake we have held validation meetings in which we have attempted this. These meetings have been attended by the teacher presenting her work, one or two of her fellow students, at least one tutor and one or two colleagues from the school in which the teacher works (and has carried out the project). I must admit, though, that assessment has been separated from validation, and it is validation that has provided critical feedback which the teacher has been able to incorporate in her final report which is marked by a tutor and seen by an external examiner.

John: Can I suggest a procedure for phase 3 based on what we did, with our third-year students? It could go something like this:

1. Participants divide into groups, and prepare statements about how they will decide whether or not they have achieved the objectives for phase 3. These objectives could be determined in part or wholly by the academic system.

2. The tutors, who should, beforehand, have formulated criteria by which they will judge a method (though these criteria would not be in the form of a model method against which the proposal is to be compared), then comment on the proposals, indicating what they like and what they dislike, and where there are procedural weaknesses which would be unacceptable.

3. The group have the chance to reformulate, and negotiate to arrive at an assessment procedure.

4. Each member of the group eventually carries out her or his self-assessment, which is tabled in detail to the group and to the tutors.

5. The self-assessment may be challenged on procedural grounds only — because it does not follow the agreed procedure, or because decisions have been made without data, or because conclusions have been reached which are not justified by what went before. But there is to be no discussion of the mark or the decision awarded (which, in our case, was contained in a sealed envelope).

6. The individual participants or students concerned may take away their assessment and redraft it, or change the decision, or make any other amendments. But the requirement is that the document eventually submitted should not be open to a valid challenge on procedural grounds.

7. Provided that requirement is met, the student's self-assessed mark or
   decision is accepted.

If your validation system should get twitchy about this, then I think it would
be possible to introduce a proviso which, for instance, might make what I have
suggested phase 4. Students who then satisfy the first three phases can receive
the normal diploma. Students who satisfy phases 1 to 4 would receive the
diploma with an addendum of the fact that the final phase of their work had
been self-directed and self-assessed.

Pamela: It's an interesting idea that could possibly be used for the interim
report in phase 3. But I would not shift from the position that tutors should be
as much involved in assessment as students, and students should be as much
involved in the development and operation of the course as tutors. Evaluation
(including assessment) should be a collaboration.

John: You are certainly dug in and well entrenched in this position where you
maintain that tutors should be as much involved in assessment as students and
that students should be as much involved in the development and operation of
the course as tutors. I am afraid that I find this a little simplistic. The
asymmetrical power relationships between tutors and students make it
doubtful how far students and tutors can be co-equally involved in
assessment; so to give students as much ownership of process as possible
within an institutional framework is important. Besides that, next year, or in
the next management situation, the teachers on your course will be on their
own; shouldn't the tutors be weaning them in preparation for that? And, in
any case, what do you mean by 'as much'? Each Wednesday my colleague and
I have a video camera aimed at us as we prepare for a workshop-style activity
with first-year students and begin to run it. In the hour that follows we replay
the video as a basis for structured recall, and we unpack what has happened
and why it happened — and we try to learn and develop, through heightened
awareness. Usually we are fortunate in having another colleague to facilitate
this for us; but if he is absent, one of us acts as a facilitator for the other, and
then we change roles. In this situation we are both engaged in the process of
formative evaluation — and I suppose you could say that we are *as much*
engaged in it as each other, because we are both as totally committed as we can
be. But that doesn't mean we share the process. Where my development, for
instance, is concerned Derek, temporarily, is my 'tutor'.

But let's get on to the whole concept of co-evaluation. I would like to see
this as facilitated evaluation. In other words, in the activities in which I have
been engaged (which are for undergraduates at third- and first-year level in a
four-year course), my job has been to facilitate the process of self-assessment. I
have seen myself as helping them to develop a philosophy and a strategy of

their own — not one which is a carbon copy of anything I would have done, or even strongly influenced by my ideas about process. I simply try to define for them the idea of comparing performance with expectations or aspirations in the context of criteria; and I try to help them to work out how they will do that objectively and rigorously, both of these terms being defined by them and judged by them and not by me or even by their peers. I can see the worth of peer interaction in the cross-fertilisation and testing of ideas. And, when they are less likely to be strongly influenced by the lecturer, I can see the advantage of a similar interaction with an academic, on some aspects of process. But co-evaluation, for me, has been a collaboration in which the self-evaluator and the facilitator have had different roles. Of course I can see that you are talking about the evaluation of an entire course rather than simply of that part of it that is the learning or development of an individual, so the lecturers must be involved — because they are then evaluating themselves.

Pamela: Most people have not got a philosophy of assessment and do not know about criteria or how to compare performance and expectations; therefore I would say that you are training your students in the skills of evaluation. When I talk about *inducting students into the procedures of formative evaluation* this is what I mean.

John: I find it difficult to believe that anyone can induct students into the procedures of formative evaluation. I would have thought that, like analysis and synthesis, this is something we've been doing since we were young children. What is required is that we go through a range of experiences which strengthen and develop our ability, and make us increasingly aware of the subtleties associated with it. We don't do this because someone inducts us into the mysteries. We learn through a series of activities which are structured and organised for us, by someone who facilitates our development.

Pamela: I don't think we are disagreeing fundamentally. I use the word *induction* because I am providing a series of activities which are organised and structured, much as the word is used to describe what goes on when a student is welcomed to a new course. Your dislike of the word 'induction' seems to stem from its positivistic associations, the idea that there is a body of knowledge into which students can be inducted. I would also reject that philosophy. I do not object to the word 'facilitation', although for me it places too much emphasis on the authority of the facilitator. I think what I want is a word that describes the way in which I can work (and learn) with students and develop alongside them.

John: Let me give an example of what I mean by facilitation. I am trying to classify the responses which I make in first-year students' learning journals at the moment. I really have four main headings, depending on my facilitative purpose. I may be trying to

1. Help the student to refine thinking which is being tabled;

2. Help the student to amplify that thinking into more breadth or depth;

3. Persuade the student that there are broader areas which have to be explored, out of which exploration something which I cannot yet predict should come;

4. Confront a writer when there seems to be a discrepancy or a lack of logic or an inconsistency in what is written, or in the comparison between what is being written and what others say or do or whatever.

At the moment more than 75% of my responses, coming from a variety of triggers (which I am having difficulty in classifying) fall into the first and fourth groups — perhaps predictably. I would anticipate that it will take until the end of the first term of a given session before something of the order of half the class are in a position to make a reasonable formative evaluation of their learning. But I think we will be disappointed if, by the end of the second term, 75% of them haven't worked out formative evaluation in their own terms — which will vary from individual to individual.

Pamela: I am extremely interested by your investigation of the comments you write on students' journals. Although my management students keep learning logs, and I have discussed these with the 1986 cohort in taped interviews, I have read only a few of them. But I did write comments on those. Next time I will consider my comments in the light of your four headings.

But it seems to me that your comments on the journals are a tactic you use to induct students into the skills of formative evaluation. Call it facilitation if you prefer, but whether it is induction or facilitation, there are dangers. Comments made by tutors and acted upon by intelligent students should result in students producing the sort of work that tutors expect. I suspect this generally means that they have learned to produce the right answer but may not know what the question was (see Gadamer, 1975; Collingwood, 1978). I would be surprised if your students are able to self-evaluate, as I understand the activity, simply as a result of your written comments. They may learn your categories and be able to apply your criteria in a fairly effective way at the end of one term, but they may not be able to move outside that.

John: Now it's my turn to burst out in a passionate and lengthy response — thereby to reveal that you touched me on a sore spot. The weakness here, I will frankly admit, is that the whole business of responses in the first-year learning journals is something that I do not yet fully understand as a process — although my experience of it associates it with significant development for the students, as they identify it and as they illustrate it by their own examples.

I probably didn't explain what I was doing sufficiently clearly. I think it's important to appreciate that I don't declare these purposes to the students. Indeed sometimes a comment will have an effect rather different from that which I intended. It's almost like the member of a congregation who reads a deep personal meaning into something said by the preacher, which the latter hadn't really intended when he prepared his sermon. The only difference is that I'm not preaching sermons, nor am I making a point in a teaching way in these marginal comments and footnotes.

Pamela: I am also guilty of not being clear enough. I recognise that you, through your comments, are interacting with the students in terms of their agendas. As I see it, the danger is the extent to which your own value position is not made explicit in your comments. My implied criticism above was that the values implicit in your comments might not be clear, and the students might get the idea that your comments were somehow 'correct' and take them over uncritically.

John: Perhaps I should give an example before I go on to my long response. Sometimes I will ask the writer if he or she can think of an example — the trigger in my mind being that the writer's thinking might thereby be amplified. To my surprise the writer in such circumstances will often discover, through the example, a completely new topic worthy of exploration. Sometimes I take the reasoning advanced by a writer and point out that the conclusion of that would be . . . (such and such). And I then ask 'Is it?' And here again the outcome for the learner is not really predictable at the time of writing the comment, because it is personal.

The learning journal, as used by my first-year students, is absolutely central to the process of personal development for them, and in this the weekly commenting is also regarded by them as crucial. Indeed it is of interest that several students from last year's first year approached me, either asking if they could keep a journal voluntarily in their second year or declaring how much they missed the weekly period for reflection and the opportunity to chew over questions and comments which were given back to them. So: (1) the students don't learn my categories — because my comments are made as a genuine response to a trigger, but without being directive. When they *are* directive, I don't see them being effective; (2) I don't think the students apply my criteria in a fairly effective way at the end of thc first term, but they begin to develop their own interpretation of the implicit criteria. What happens then is that, at the beginning of the second term, we ask these 17- and 18-year-olds to draw up their own criteria by which they will judge their journal work in the second term. Then we use these criteria as the framework within which to show them our comparison, to match up against their own. So that's a neat reversal of the allocation which you have been reporting. In our case the students select the criteria, each student makes her or his own comparison, and we follow *their* process. If our written value judgement conveys the same message as that formulated by the student, then we accept the student one.

Pamela: And if not? And how is this different from my phase 1 assessment? But the interesting thing for me is that although I could use your four headings for writing comments about my own students' work, I could not use them to apply to your students' work. This is because the important theory/practice link is implicit in your comments. I suggest that it is a heading that is missing and should be put in your scheme.

John: Asking the students to square up what they have learned with what they have practised is my category 4 (if I suspect there is going to be a misfit), or my category 1 (if I believe that there is good agreement but something worthwhile to be learnt from the comparison), or my category 2 or 3 in other circumstances. It depends on the trigger.

Pamela: Are you saying that all your comments relate to the theory/practice dimension? If not, you have buttonholed the point I am making. Theory/ practice is implicit in your thinking and needs to be made explicit. I could use the four categories for my comments on my students' work because I would also be very concerned implicitly with the theory/practice link. I would not have similar implicit understanding if I was making comment for your students. Do you see what I mean?

When it comes to validating your categories, you would seem to be quite advanced in being able to compare them with the criteria that students construct to judge their second term learning journals. But what about peer and professional validation? There surely must be a *specialist* category that would differentiate between the comments suitable for your engineering students and the comments suitable for my schoolteachers?

John: I think something has gone wrong when you come to this question about validating my categories. The categories that my peers would employ emerge from, for example, transactional analysis. The categories that my students would employ would relate to their responses and not to the reasons which led me to make my comments. And as for the teaching profession, I have difficulty in finding many people who make this kind of facilitative comment, and none of these have got beyond the stage of doing it intuitively — whereas we want to sharpen our awareness of why we are doing things and perhaps of what outcomes may be.

Pamela: Perhaps I am luckier than you because my involvement in action research has introduced me to a small number of people who have been examining their own practice in much the way that you have been doing. What we share is a commitment to the educational value of improving the practice of teaching and through this improving students' learning.

John: I liked the discussion in your paper of the reason why the value basis of evaluation has not always been recognised. Alan Harding and I have found it helpful to take the value out of evaluation for a while, and use the term (to please the world) to describe the assembling and analysis of data. We then point out that where the values come in is in making decisions about what that analysis says to you. All three activities, of course, are part of the grand total of evaluation; it's just unfortunate that the world doesn't use the vocabulary that way. I hope that's clear — because I'm really trying to say that I agree with what you've written and have expressed part of it in a different way elsewhere. (Cowan & Harding, 1986).

Pamela: I think there is another interesting issue related to values and evaluation. There is a lot of research to suggest that teachers (at all levels) deny their values in their practice. In fact this is the position from which Jack Whitehead, and the schoolteachers with whom he works, embark on action research into their own practice (Whitehead, 1985c). How do you cope with the fact that people will claim they hold certain values and then deny these values in their practices? I think it is a crucial issue when one is getting students to make contracts about their own learning.

John: If I am being totally genuine, my immediate reaction is that this person who holds values and then denies them in practice is probably me. But I doubt if you could shift me simply by telling me that I am a hypocrite. I am ashamed to admit that will probably push me into a position in which I will passionately defend my actions, and probably believe that I am being misunderstood or misjudged. You must find a way in which you hold up a mirror or play back a tape recorder (literally or metaphorically) or encourage me to test out my values in a variety of developing situations until *I* discover, privately and in a supporting environment, that there is an inconsistency of which I am ashamed and which I wish to change. That's not, maybe, the *only* way to do it, but it's the only way I know. It works for me when someone caringly facilitates me in that style. And, so far, it has worked for me when I have genuinely tried to help someone else to come to grips with inconsistency and have identified with them as they felt the hurt and strived to emerge from it. If I am facilitator in such circumstances, this is not something I do to someone — it is something I do *with* someone, where my role is to help them to appreciate an outside perspective and hence move towards self-awareness.

Pamela: I think you have just described what I mean by course evaluation as action research. And you have certainly placed the tutor squarely at the centre of the process!

11 Working together towards a better understanding of the primary classroom

PAT BROADHEAD

This paper focuses upon stage 2 of a three-stage research project undertaken with funding from an ESRC (Economic and Social Research Council) studentship. The project has explored primary teachers' working perceptions of 'good practice'. It sought to expose their professional understandings of classroom life by engaging teachers in reflective dialogue in support of Schon's premise that competent practitioners usually know more than they can say (Schon, 1983). Teachers were subsequently encouraged to reveal something of the realities they perceive themselves facing on a daily basis and to review the potential those realities have for constraining or enhancing daily practice. Further, it sought to explore the potential for incorporating teachers' professional understandings of classroom life into existing theory whilst withstanding imputations regarding the validity of professional knowledge.

We currently know little about the ways in which teachers create their theoretical constructs, or about how the classroom images they retain once an event is passed impinge upon and contribute towards the pedagogical basis for their daily practice. Classroom-based research should perhaps be seeking to create a framework within which teachers might purposefully seek enhancement of practice by better understanding of the basis for classroom action.

The three-stage methodology: (1) informal interview; (2) classroom observation; and (3) filming the classroom, was initially identified as an appropriate sequence for data collection in order to disclose pedagogical theory building. At stage 2, when the researcher spent a week in each of six teachers' classrooms, the teachers came to regularly address fundamental issues pertaining to teaching and learning, in the company of the researcher. These reflective acts demanded an analytical assessment that increasingly prompted teachers to question or celebrate the validity of their own actions within a context of children learning.

This chapter will outline research methodology at stage 2 and explore relationships between insider and outsider. The partnerships were to reveal initial tensions as teachers inevitably confronted the possibility of the outsider taking a judgemental stance. Yet this preliminary tension was rapidly offset as opportunities for reflective articulations disclosed the positive attributes of insider/outsider partnerships for revealing across-case insights of professional theory building to the outsider and insights pertaining to personal practice to the insider.

Methodology

Stage 1 consisted of informal interviews. These constituted discussions with 22 primary teachers from six schools adjudged challenging in which to teach (the basis for school selection related to prevailing social and environmental factors). The teachers taught across the age range 3–13. Each teacher was offered three questions to consider several days prior to the $1-1\frac{1}{2}$ hour interview; this promoted comparability across cases without sacrificing a relaxed forum for informal discussion.

The three questions asked teachers:

a. to recall four or five instances when 'things had gone well in the classroom';

b. to recall occasions or periods of time when they believed their practice had changed;

c. to recall instances when they had felt themselves to be having difficulties with their practice.

Data suggested that whilst all 22 teachers could recall instances of good practice, their pedagogical understanding of the factors which promoted those instances showed some variance. Constructs pertaining to the identification of 'good practice', a capacity to act on such constructs and professional development emerged as inter-related strands.

It was apparent that some teachers had gradually become curious as to why children were not learning as efficiently as they had initially thought they would, and they had gradually become bold enough to explore the possibility that the child's difficulties might be founded in their own teaching strategies rather than in the child's relative ability to learn. The curiosity and the emboldened behaviour seemingly correlated with a perceived need to innovate or to initiate change within the existing patterns of organisation and educational provision. Subsequently, their considerations of 'good practice' were implicitly related to their explanation and evaluation of the periods of observed practice.

Stage 2 consisted of classroom observation. The research moved into six primary classrooms, three in first schools and three in middle schools with the researcher taking the role of non-participant observer and the teachers continuing to offer insights into their perceptions of good practice and the basis for their own practice.

Stage 3 involved filming two teachers and asking them to offer reflective comment. The films depict life in the classrooms over a two-day period, with additional material filmed two terms later at the teachers' request. The original material was edited and the commentary scripted in consultation with the two teachers.

One film is entitled *Working with children*. The teacher, Sally, reflects on the children's actions, their progress and the environment she provides in order to sustain a self-directed learning environment. The second film is entitled *Through a primary door: thinking and talking about teaching*. Denise offers reflections on her changing practice as she introduces new ideas into the classroom which she believes will enhance the learning experiences she offers to children. Both teachers' reflections expose their pedagogical understandings and their subsequent impact on the teaching/learning ethos.

Insiders and Outsiders

Educational research has traditionally relied upon outsider data collection to furnish insights of classroom events and to theory-build. The validity of outsider perspectives within this complex environment are currently being called into question as the relevance of teachers' professional knowledge and its impact on the learning environment becomes more widely understood. Desforges & McNamara (1979) propose that because of this impact, trainee teachers should not be placed in positions whereby they acquire craft knowledge 'quickly and covertly'. Rather, they should become conscious deliberators of theory–practice links. However, Desforges & McNamara point to previous attempts to explore craft knowledge as disappointing, and in a later paper, McNamara (1980) proposes that this is largely due to outsiders having 'fail[ed] significantly to understand and appreciate the realities of classroom life as seen from the point of view of the practitioner'. He points to existing findings as being more indicative of the values and perspectives of the educational researcher than of the factors which shape teacher behaviour.

Zeichner *et al.* (1987) examine a variety of individual and social influences on the development of teachers' craft knowledge and point to a number of related studies which are concerned to make explicit the complex, practically orientated and socially derived perspectives through which teachers direct the work of teaching. Professional knowledge is gradually being revealed as incompatible with a deficit model of teaching. Brown & McIntyre (1986) argue that in-service education should emulate a sharing model wherein teachers build on their strengths to effect professional enhancement of practice. As Calderhead argues (1987), until teachers have access to a language and concepts which realistically represent their classroom practice and acknowledge the complexity of their work, the potential of such a model for successful implementation is diminished.

My research was conceived to address such issues. It proposed in so doing to take specific account of insider/outsider gulfs. A fundamental premise which underpinned the research from the outset and guided the outsider as she strove to establish equally weighted, interactive relationships with insiders was founded in Schon's arguments (Schon, 1983). He maintains that uncertainties, far from being external indicators of a need for professional progress, are the potential basis for enhanced effectiveness. They constitute a positive and inevitable facet of classroom life wherein teachers who recognise them as such are able to accept the challenge of implementing new strategies whilst simultaneously acknowledging and assimilating revised pedagogies. Enhanced practice is founded on perceived wisdom, not accounted deficiencies.

It was this premise, along with a perceived need to understand further why primary teachers acted as they did, which prompted the researcher to pursue a basis for partnership that would differ from the action research paradigm in terms of who would determine the focus and how data would be interpreted, but which, like the action research paradigm, would give priority to reflection on action as a significant source of teacher knowledge.

Carr & Kemmis (1986) are highly critical of applied research conducted by academic researchers who claim action research status but who merely co-opt practitioners into gathering data about educational practices for them. They refer to projects 'not in teachers' hands'. This difficulty was similarly confronted by Elliot (1985) in describing a team of facilitators who noted, as the project was under way, that teachers were reluctant to accept someone else's problem definitions as conditions of their participation. True action research, according to Carr & Kemmis (1986), is concerned with the systematic investigation of a social or educational practice, is participatory or collaborative and promotes a spiral of self-reflection.

My research accommodated an outsider-determined focus; it incorporated outsider-initiated methodology for eliciting data. It became increasingly collaborative at stages 2 and 3 in that at stage 2, teachers were the significant identifiers of the agenda for reflective debate and at stage 3, the two teachers involved in the filming and editing process took a significant lead in determining both the content of the films and the means of sharing them with other practitioners. My research did support Carr & Kemmis' concept of the applicability of the reflective spiral in terms of teacher professional development. Detailed analysis of all reflective data demonstrated that teachers intent on enhancing their current teaching condition perceived themselves as being, figuratively speaking, on a journey somewhere, rather than endeavouring to attain a plateau-like state of 'good teacherhood'.

My research did not incorporate systematic opportunities for teachers to identify and pursue a personally determined focus, and Nixon (1981) proposes that this lies at the heart of action research. Rather than defining teachers' perceived problems as a basis for practitioner action it was intent on liberating theory–practice links across cases. This seemed to hold instant appeal for teachers as they affirmed that yes, it was time someone asked *them* what constituted good practice.

It was also inappropriate for the researcher to consider adopting the role of 'trusted outsider' at stage 2 (Cummings & Hustler, 1986). In action research all those involved in the research process should come to participate equally in planning, acting, observing and reflecting (Carr & Kemmis, 1986). This was the model that Cummings & Hustler endeavoured to adopt. In my research, the planning and observing were the sole prerogative of the outsider; the acting the prerogative of the insider and the reflective insights mainly the prerogative of the insider with the outsider occasionally stimulating recall by asking questions about specific instances she had observed and about which she wanted to know more. As the week progressed, teachers invariably referred to the impact of these reflective dialogues on their day-to-day practice, claiming that they enabled them to clarify their daily basis for action and evaluate its appropriateness in terms of future action. The researcher was increasingly forced to acknowledge the impact of her presence on each teacher's confrontation with uncertainty and certainty of action. It was also evident that if she were to ask teachers to confront uncertainty, in the company of an outsider, she must offer respect and support on the occasions when teachers seemed less than pleased with their practice. Undoubtedly each teacher's capacity to share their understandings about day-to-day practice and its impact on the teaching/learning ethos contributed to the drawing together of inter-related, emergent theoretical strands and facilitated the gradual development of a reflective framework for promoting the exploration of the current teaching condition.

The basis for data collection at this stage of the research was teacher reflection on classroom events in order to elicit perspectives on good practice, what form it takes, how it is initiated and the role the teachers see for themselves and for the child as contributors to progress. The observer had to be aware of the events in order to understand fully and locate teacher reflections within a set of shared experiences. If the observer were to take the role of 'second-teacher', not only would she be initiating other events outside the class teacher's domain, she also ran the risk of becoming so engrossed in the second-teacher/pupil interactions which would follow that she would not always be in a position to witness class teacher/pupil interaction. If the teacher subsequently chose to reflect on such incidents in the focus on good practice, the researcher could not legitimately claim to be in a position to complement the reflective articulations with observational notes. This ultimately came to be a significant means of validating and sharing the professional reflections of these teachers.

Insiders work in the school and are intimate with its ethos; they have developed relationships with pupils in their class and in other classes, with the head, colleagues and parents. Their response to the school ethos and the nature of those relationships cannot be predicted. Each teacher has a singular relationship with their primary class and may occasionally perceive a colleague or the head as an 'outsider', unknowing of their innermost aspirations and intentions. Outsiders work outside the school, initially knowing nothing of the ethos; nor do they have relationships in any of the above categories, although these may be developed. The outsider enters the school to discover the nature of these aspects; the purposes for developing ethos awareness or 'insider' relationships are likely to differ from those of the class teacher, although both insiders and outsiders soon learn that they must know of these in order to survive. It is their use of the knowledge, once attained, that causes them to remain insiders or outsiders. Traditionally, in all research but action research the outsider has taken knowledge away in the form of data; the insider remains *in situ* with their knowledge.

I entered the classroom as an outsider who gave priority to combining authentic enquiry with respect for professional knowledge. I increasingly strove to act on the premise that researchers cannot suspend their responsibilities in terms of fellow professionals' personal and professional development by citing a need for objectivity as the disclaimer. It was as stage 2 unfolded that I found myself confronting the full implications and acknowledging the accompanying responsibilities.

Watching, Talking and Listening to Teachers

Both the researcher and the practitioner brought complementary attributes to the research project. These were identified as follows:

The researcher brought:

the focus;

the reserves to sustain the focus;

her skills as a non-participant observer; and

the professional knowledge elicited from other practitioners.

The teacher brought:

a willingness to be involved;

a capacity to reflect on action;

a cumulative store of professional knowledge; and

a personal understanding of the teaching/learning experiences ongoing in their classroom.

The following section intends to address these attributes as paired headings in order to exemplify their complementary status.

The focus – a willingness to be involved

Unlike stage 1 research, no predetermined questions, however loosely structured, were incorporated into stage 2. These discussions usually began with a casually worded invitation from the researcher to the teacher to 'Tell me about what you were pleased with today'. However, an inter-related model was emerging, founded on the reflective articulations of the 22 teachers involved in stage 1 and offering insights into the ways in which primary teachers think about their classrooms and the links with pedagogical theory building. The model was being explored within a framework which had identified ten questions which it seemed primary teachers would inevitably confront when they become intent on enhancing their practice. This model and the questions offered a significant focus for interactive dialogue as the researcher sought to encourage the teachers to explicate their basis for action whilst endeavouring to avoid closed questions and to continue facilitating the revelation of personally held teacher preoccupations and celebrations.

It was evident from the outset to both teachers and researcher that teacher participation would make considerable demands on teacher time. Discussions usually took place at lunch-time and at day's end, occasions when the teacher might usually be relaxing or preparing. Each conversation would last between 30 minutes and one hour, and was recorded. At the end of the week, each teacher was asked to make a written response to the experience. An offer of classroom cover whilst teachers engaged in this always accompanied the request.

One teacher, Denise, made a very salutary comment when first asked if time might be spent in her classroom. She remarked: 'I know what you're doing, you're coming to see if what I say I do in the classroom is what I really do, aren't you?' (Denise: First school). Such was the nature of the relationship on the basis of the initial interview that she felt entitled to confront the researcher with a question which surely preoccupies any teacher asked by an educational researcher if they 'might enter your classroom'. As the researcher worded her response it became apparent that there existed an inherent need to account not only to the teachers, but to the educational world at large for the supposedly non-judgemental nature of the research. Seeking as this research did to offer an alternative to prescriptive models of good practice, it became increasingly apparent that good relationships would be maintained only if teachers remained convinced that the research gave priority to their working knowledge.

Non-participant observers seek non-threatening anonymity in the classroom. Their potential for attaining this state rests on their capacity to manifest some credibility in terms of classroom knowledge and to demonstrate empathy with the teacher's classroom realities and responsibilities. The onus is upon the researchers to show they do understand classrooms but that they seek to understand them more, rather than on the teacher to demonstrate that they are worthy of attention.

It seemed important to create an opportunity for addressing Denise's question with each of the six teachers before classroom observations began, although no other teacher asked it quite as specifically as she had done. It was also evident that the relationship building which had taken place before and during informal interviews was a continuing contributor during stage 2. The researcher had sought to put teachers at their ease before the interviews by briefly referring to her own, fairly recent, work as a primary teacher. Generally, teachers had been quite interested in the route that had led this once 'insider' to her current occupation as researcher and seemed to perceive the transition as a verification of teacher knowledge rather than a desertion of the ranks.

As each teacher was approached to invite their continuing participation, the researcher deliberately sought to create an opportunity for discussing the role of the outsider as classroom observer. She emphasised partnership in working together to uncover the day-to-day processes that led teachers to be as they were. The format was much the same for all six classes. The researcher would position herself discreetly and record the teacher's and the children's actions, detailing comments or questions to ask at a later stage.

One strategy was abandoned in the early days of stage 2. Initially teachers were asked to note incidents or instances they would like to discuss during the post-teaching reflections. Teachers seemed to find this difficult. The act of writing, albeit brief note-making, seemed an intrusion into the act of teaching, interrupting the flow and disturbing the momentum needed to sustain interactions with children. Teachers were required to 'break off' in order to engage in an act they did not seem to perceive as being relevant. The act of teaching may be about communication rather than introspective reflection. It is interesting to speculate, however, that had this been an action research project with a teacher-determined research focus, the teachers may have considered such note-taking to be relevant, useful and worth the commitment in time.

The reserves to sustain the focus – a capacity to reflect on action

The solitary classroom observer is engaged in a relatively lonely business as she deflects attempts at interaction from children without seeming surly and hostile (a wholly inappropriate response by any adult in an educational setting); as she withholds her help from a struggling child, directing him to peers or to the teacher; and as she endeavours to seem alert and interested at all times when the reality is that she is hungry, thirsty or even bored with the proceedings. Primary classrooms are not generally noted for high drama, but rather for a buzz and hum of activity that follows much the same pattern from day to day. However, the high points were not only the theatre performance by a visiting group or the chance to share in wine and chocolates at a member of staff's birthday. They also took the form of conversations with one headteacher who shared, at length, her concerns and difficulties in endeavouring to promote a child-centred learning environment, her growing belief over many years that this was the only way to teach and her struggles to convince her own doubting inner voice and her peers and superiors that she was right to pursue this goal. The reserves were also sustained by occasional letters from teachers with whom I had already spent time; letters which seemed to indicate that they continued to engage in the reflective process and in which they raised issues and ideas directly related to and with the capacity to extend my own emerging thoughts.

It would be difficult to offer in this chapter extensive examples of the six teachers' respective capacities to reflect on action. The following examples offer some insights into two significant threads that emerged from teacher reflections:

a. the way in which personally held theories impinge on practice as teachers search for certainty of action; and

b. the ways in which teachers see the realities of classroom life as having the potential to constrain good practice, but by engaging with those realities the teacher creates an opportunity to enhance learning experiences.

In this first extract, Sheila proffers her constructs on the turning of rhetoric into practice with her endeavours to create a meaningful learning experience for children:

All the things we are after in their learning need to come slowly. It's not time wasted. Time spent now is time saved later. You can see the dividends it pays later on. It helps the learning process and makes it easier for them because they become independent learners. They don't always need a teacher to tell them what to do. They need to see learning as a whole, to see the progression. I think we're guilty as teachers of having our objectives in our own head, but we don't convey this to the children and they don't understand why we're doing certain things. It's important to tell them this is part of a whole scheme. (Sheila: Middle school)

In this second extract, as John reflects on his own and a child's actions, it is also possible to glimpse something of the basis for his response to the situation:

I was pleased with the effect in the classroom that the group work was having. Then there was the little altercation between Kevin and the rest of the group. He is new to the school and his history has been one of turmoil. I thought we were going to get a flashpoint situation at one stage. I wondered about just leaving it and then I thought 'No'. This was

a situation that had to be resolved there and then, otherwise it might
grow. I spent time talking to Kevin about his problem. I thought the rest
of the class ought to hear what Kevin had to say to be able to understand
him. They could see the potential problem he has working with others.
(John: Middle school)

Teacher reflections are the focus of my research; the underlying premise that
personal theories impinge upon and shape classroom practice is explored and
substantiated with insiders' reflective comment and outsider's observational
notes. These six teachers were approached because their reflections at stage 1
had shown them as unwilling to rely on serendipity (a fortuitous accident from
which progress is made) but instead to go in search of a greater certainty of
practice. The term 'serendipity' was introduced to the research by Louise, at
stage 1, as she comments upon another tenet that was to emerge as influential
in terms of professional development — coping with the unexpected. She
reflects:

Louise: I think too there are the serendipity occasions when really good things
have happened in the classroom, but you're not expecting them.

Pat: Can you recall one of those?

Louise: At the moment, we're watching a programme 'The Boy from Space'
and basing a good deal of work around it. I had initial fears that it wouldn't be
context bound but it has lent itself to an enormous number of context bound
situations. Because a lot of the children are learning English as a second
language I would read the chapter through before we saw the programme and
get children to explain the plot in mother tongue. Chapter four dealt with the
Boy from Space appearing in the sandpit and coming toward the two
characters, trying to communicate. He is pale and frightened and the children
in the story cannot understand what he is saying. The response from the
children was incredible. It touched on something they had experienced so
deeply that they knew how the boy felt. It released an enormous amount of
memories: 'I do remember feeling like that; it was lovely to get home where
people were speaking Bengali.' That kind of experience just comes up and I
think it has deepened our relationship. (Louise: First school)

Reflections from other teachers were to substantiate the premise that such
experiences will deepen relationships only when teachers recognise their
potential for so doing. Under such circumstances, the unexpected sustains its
potential for shaping future practice.

Skills as a non-participant observer – a cumulative store of professional knowledge

The non-participant observer seeks anonymity. Threats to this can take several forms. One teacher asked me not to wear a red dress again as it continually caught her eye as she looked around the room. It was evident that if I sat in direct line of eye contact, teachers were momentarily distracted, as if suddenly recalling the presence of another adult. It seemed important to maintain a low profile in the classroom and respond naturally to any overtures teachers might make. It would have been ill-conceived to consign these overtures to a category of relative unimportance. It seemed that teachers were endeavouring to determine what role this outsider would take. Four teachers introduced me to the children, two did not. In the latter cases, children asked about my presence. John made it clear that children were not to approach the observer for help and explained this later by saying: 'At this stage, I'm trying to encourage them to get on without always referring to an adult'.

Other teachers chose, in the earlier stages, to approach me as I observed, and explain the basis for the learning experiences I was watching them initiate and maintain. My response was to listen without prompting debate, and the regularity of such instances diminished. Each teacher invited a response from me at whole group discussion times, on a variety of topics ranging from birthdays, family, the car I drove and the schools in which I had taught. This strategy seemed to be a blend of polite interaction with a fellow adult and a desire to know how this fellow adult talked to children and how much she would reveal about herself, a testing of her credentials.

The classroom observation notes were available to teachers to read. All the teachers glanced once at these and after noting their predominantly factual nature with accompanying researcher comments and questions scribbled in the adjacent column, they seemed little interested.

Inevitably there were incidents in the classroom, that the researcher with no teaching responsibilities could observe at much greater leisure than the teacher. Such instances were often described to the teacher, especially when the teacher's reflections indicated marginal awareness. One particular incident in Sally's room was interesting in this context.

Sally and Denise team teach six- and seven-year-olds in adjoining units; Timothy is new to the unit. Sally and Denise had a well discussed and mutual policy of allowing Timothy to explore this new environment. He had previously experienced a very different school setting and was unused to the freedom of choice. Sally frequently spoke of her concern to focus Timothy's attention for a length of time, although she suspected that 'he is very bright underneath all that floating around'.

One day, I observed Timothy as he wandered around the classroom, chatting to other children. They told him what they were doing and he watched. He watched two children playing a game and then fetched a pencil. He was meant to be measuring and cutting strips of paper as part of his science work. He took a pencil, walked away then returned; tipped out the pencils and began to rearrange them in order of size. He remained engrossed for three or four minutes. A child came for a pencil and Timothy explained what he was doing. The child watched. Timothy finally returned the pencils to the box. He drew one line on his paper and went to the paper cutter. He placed his pencil line against the edge of the cutter and cut his first strip. He began to cut a second strip but did not measure it. Sally had earlier explained to the class how to ensure that each strip was the same size and demonstrated how to use the paper cutter. A boy came to use the cutter and watched Timothy. At his second attempt, Timothy did not place his paper against the top edge of the cutter and tried to push the guarded blade away from himself. The cutter will not work if used in this way. The boy kneeled beside Timothy. Timothy bent down and looked at the blade, he turned the cutter around, the boy put his weight on the card over the paper and together they succeeded in cutting a second piece. Timothy compared the two and found they differed in size; they chatted about this. He studied briefly, commented again to the boy and then laid his first strip against the paper, drew a line and immediately cut a second piece. After this he cut several more pieces and with them in his hand, proceeded to wander again around the classroom. He had spent nearly ten minutes at the paper cutter.

When this observation was shared with Sally, she was surprised at the extent of Timothy's commitment to task. She in turn shared it with Denise and each maintained that from that point, they would see Timothy 'in a new light'.

The reasons for offering this story are twofold. Firstly, it indicates the extent of the opportunity Timothy was offered to find out about his environment. Sally had said this was her intention and indeed this seemed evident from his behaviour, although Sally was not specifically sure as to how Timothy was using his time and had been concerned at his seemingly slow progress. Secondly, it suggests that being offered insights of such incidents by the observer, in order to elicit reflective comment, will have an impact on the teacher's understanding of classroom life. It seemed purposeless and ungracious to withhold information of this sort on the basis that it might 'colour' the research. It was considered slight return for being allowed into the classroom and it seemed evident that the teacher's response to instances such as these were an integral and illuminating part of the reflective experience in which they were being asked, by the outsider, to engage.

After the classrooms observations were completed, Sally wrote:

During the course of the week, I often made comments like: 'I didn't get much done'. But by sitting after the children had gone and reflecting and assessing the work, I was able to see the progress of individuals. Having another pair of eyes in the room showed up some good points. As I scan the area, I often miss important areas of learning. I didn't see Timothy use the large cutter.

Denise also wrote:

Having Pat in the room and knowing what she was observing made me more aware of those aspects myself. It was great to find out what Timothy does all day. I found myself doing a bit more observing. It has led Sally and me to think about the value of more detailed and regular discussions of wider aspects of classroom management.

The cumulative store of professional knowledge which all the teachers participating in the three stages of this research evidenced, to one degree or another, has contributed significantly to the development of a reflective framework designed to promote the exploration of the current teaching condition. 'What do I know about my teaching; how did I become this teacher and where is my teaching going?' have emerged as important questions in the enhancement of practice and the perception of self as engaged in a developmental journey alongside children.

Professional knowledge from other practitioners – personal understanding of the classroom

The model and ten questions founded in and substantiated by teacher reflection are mentioned above. This emerging theory would constitute an integral facet of the researcher's professional baggage as she entered the six primary classrooms intent on extending the theoretical strands that were emerging by founding them in reflections on current rather than recalled practice, which had formed the basis of stage 1. The teachers' professional baggage continued to be their working knowledge and familiarity with a classroom situation and with children relatively unknown to the outsider.

It was a salutary reminder of their special knowledge that teachers often cited instances of good practice as being those occasions when individual children made particular progress in the classroom:

One of the main things I was most pleased about was little Afsal. He contributed to the group as we were talking. He told us about something that he had noticed. For Afsal to do that in the context of what was going on was, to me, quite tremendous. It was a big breakthrough. Afsal normally switches off. At the moment he's under review for the most appropriate kind of education. (John: Middle school)

I feel that I'm able to relax a bit more. It's beginning to work. Little things like David came in and took the pencils away at the end of the lesson. Normally he would have had to say 'Can I take the pencils?', but he just did it. (Sheila: Middle school)

Abid counted to six without faltering. Considering he's had two weeks off, that's pretty good going. He does have a lot of time off because of illness and he often forgets what he's done. We spend so much time revising that he doesn't seem to get any further. He could also split six into four and two, so tomorrow I'll stretch him a bit further, really extend him while I've got him. Hopefully he'll come tomorrow. (Rachel: First school)

Progress for individual children seemed particularly important in a context of good practice; not knowing the children as well as the teacher did it would have been impossible for the outsider to note progress of this sort. These kinds of teacher assessments seem to constitute a crucial basis for future action in that teachers give priority to building upon the achievements of individuals. There were also occasions when a teacher's reflective comments dimensionally extended what seemed to the outsider to be an uneventful observational episode. Teachers would disclose the impact of provision and strategies on specific developmental needs focused upon by themselves during the interaction on the basis of what they perceived themselves as knowing about an individual child.

Where should Partnerships Lead?

Both during and after stage 2, teachers indicated the quite substantial impact of 'getting into the habit' of reflecting. Rachel remarked:

It helped me to look at my practice by having you at the back of the room because although I'm not that aware of you, I'll stand up and think: 'Well, why am I standing up now?' Often you just realise that there's a need for organisation at some point so that children can move on. (Rachel: First school)

John, a colleague in the adjoining Middle school, embarked on a year's secondment shortly after the observation period, to explore a school-based commission within the authority's school-focused development programme. Our paths crossed one day and as we chatted, he remarked how helpful to his current work he had found the 'reflective habit' in that it sustained a discipline which offered insights into his own and colleagues' practice.

Denise was asked by her headteacher to offer school-based in-service training to her colleagues in connection with her responsibilities for reading in the school. She negotiated with her colleagues a role as non-participant observer followed by a two-way dialogue similar to that she had experienced. She remarked: 'In 15 years of teaching, you were the first non-threatening person that has ever sat in my classroom, watched me work and listened to me talk. It helped me so much, that I just felt I wanted to offer that to others' (Denise: First school).

In presenting data, I have subsequently sought to combine observational notes with specific reflective comment and offer insights into the theoretical basis for decisions about daily practice.

It may appear something of a contradiction in terms to talk on the one hand about generalisable theory and on the other about personal theoretical frameworks. Their complementary facets have become more apparent as the research has progressed. The challenge of drawing the concepts closer together, with teacher reflections as the central tenet, has facilitated the emergence of a reflective model of classroom life which has endeavoured to avoid prescription, confront realities and retain the potential to promote enhanced practice. The research has offered me some comprehensive insights into the ways in which primary teachers interpret classroom action; both their own and the child's. It has revealed some interesting teacher insights into classroom life; insights which it seems, in the light of teacher reflection, enable teachers to evaluate ongoing action and form the basis of future practice. The research has striven to ensure that such insights are not only conveyed at anecdotal level, but also that teachers' potential to generate as well as uphold theories of teaching and learning is revealed. It seems that in order to encourage teachers to empower themselves with the potential to do this, the outsiders should be utilising their skills in the search for perspectives which are meaningful to teachers — this they can surely only do in conjunction with teachers.

Research methodologies must enable teachers to contribute as equal partners rather than attempt analysis and categorisation of their teaching strategies out of context of their personal theories. Teachers should not perceive themselves as being 'acted upon' by an outside agent, neither should they be encouraged to perceive uncertainties as indicators of bad or weak practice. Classroom researchers and classroom practitioners have complementary skills and should employ them in partnership, if there is to be a better understanding of primary classroom life.

Perhaps, in the past, there has not been full acknowledgement that, by entering a teacher's classroom, the researcher has engaged with the teacher in a one-to-one exchange of knowledge; the informal and formal interactions alert the teacher to a more intensive awareness about their classrooms and their practice. The teacher in turn contributes to the outsider's professional understanding by offering insights, professional knowledge and theoretical constructs which the outsider, generally 'out of touch' with the day-to-day demands of class teaching, can accommodate within their existing frames of reference of a wider range of classrooms, ways of working and theories of teaching and learning than is likely to be available to the teacher whose priority must always be, in educational terms, the advancement of the children in their care. We have yet to explore fully the potential of the teacher–researcher liaison for the sharing of knowledge.

12 Making sense of reality: A case study of one teacher reflecting on her practice

HUGH BUSHER

This case study explores how one inexperienced teacher talked about her work and her experiences in school as she watched a video recording of herself teaching a lesson. June developed explanations for a diverse range of activities in her classroom, and for the links between what happened in her classroom and the culture of the rest of the school and the social environment in which the school was located.

The Research Project

For the last two years, I have been exploring how inexperienced teachers think about their practices by observing their lessons and talking with them afterwards about the thinking that lies behind their intentions, actions and points of view and about the sources of their pedagogy.

June was a teacher of mathematics in a suburban comprehensive school. She was one of a cohort of nine teachers — four male and five female — with whom we worked for the academic year 1986/87. The word 'worked' is used here because it would be inaccurate to claim that we collaborated with them, as in an action research programme — not least because the teachers did not determine the agenda of the research. On the other hand, at the end of the year, several of the teachers commented on how the process of being observed and videoed and of talking about their classroom practices had made them more explicitly aware of what was happening in their classrooms. Further, their concerns and experiences heightened our awareness of how we did and should carry out research, particularly of the moral and ethical dilemmas involved therein.

The teachers came from a variety of subject backgrounds, but they all taught in secondary schools in the urban areas of West Yorkshire. They had all been PGCE students at the University of Leeds at some time since 1982. Although this link gave us our initial contact with our co-workers we still had to negotiate entry to their classrooms, and relied on their help in negotiating entry to their schools.

With each teacher we carried out a semi-structured initial interview to reveal the teacher's professional biography, and to find out how they saw their work in school. We also asked them from where they felt they had learned their ideas and practices. This issue of the source of their ideas often re-emerged during post-lesson discussions (see below) when the teachers were commenting on the interactions that had taken place during their lessons and on the institutional context in which these had occurred.

To provide a focus for discussion about the process of teaching, we observed each of our co-workers teaching three lessons with one class of her/ his own choice. These lessons were immediately prior to a break in a teacher's teaching programme so that we could talk after the lesson. In these post-lesson discussions teachers were encouraged to describe and comment on what they thought had been happening during the lesson, and to explain why they had acted in certain ways in certain situations. We were consciously non-judgemental during these discussions, as we wished to explore the teachers' interpretations of the interactions which had occurred.

With all our co-workers, including June, the first two lessons were recorded with observers' notes and audio tape-recorder. This was to keep the non-participant observer's profile as low as possible — 'fly on the wall' approach — whilst accustoming the pupils to the presence of an observer. The observer's notes were used in the post-lesson discussions to remind teacher and observer about what events had taken place. The post-lesson discussion was tape-recorded and transcribed, and copies of the transcription given to the teacher. This was intended to give the teacher opportunity to reflect on the transcript and add further comment by written note or during a later discussion if s/he so desired. In fact only two co-workers took this opportunity, and then only to make textual emendations, such as substituting 'taught' for 'talked'.

The third lesson was video-recorded, using a single camera with a wide angle lens to capture as broad a view of the action as possible. No artificial lighting was used and only one camera crew. As well as resolving the technical, intellectual and ethical problems of having to edit the video recording before replaying it to teacher and observer at a subsequent meeting, making video recordings in this way helped to minimise the obtrusiveness of the observer in the classroom environment. To allow the camera to capture as much of the lesson interaction as possible, it was positioned towards the front of the class. This had the disadvantage of increasing its visibility to the pupils but the advantage of allowing the camera crew to record the expressions on the pupils' faces as well as those on the teacher's face.

The video recording was used to create a stimulated post-lesson discussion. Such discussions often took place several days after the recording had been made. They were usually held at the University of Leeds, neutral territory for the teachers. As in the post-lesson discussions, the teacher was encouraged to comment on what was seen happening in the video recording and on the institutional context in which it occurred. The reviewing of a single lesson often took over two hours for an hour-long lesson. Even then it was often not possible to review the whole lesson, without 'fast-forwarding' at least part of it. We felt it was important, ethically, to allow the teachers to see the complete record of their lessons. In June's case, at her request, this stimulated post-lesson discussion took place at her school in an empty classroom after the end of the school day.

In addition to discussion with our co-workers, we sometimes interviewed their heads of department and/or other senior teachers to find out about the parts öur co-workers played in their schools and in their departments. This posed a particularly delicate ethical dilemma for maintaining the anonymity of all the participants interviewed in the same school. For various reasons that are relevant to discussions on how and why researchers modify their practices, but not to this chapter, we were not able to do this in every school. In June's school, I interviewed her head of department some time after I had finished working with June.

We also tried out group interviews with our co-workers. On two occasions we brought together as many of the entire year's cohort as wanted to meet. We expected this to provide us with an interesting exchange of views between people in different schools and hoped that our co-workers would take the opportunity to begin to establish a support network for themselves. The first aim was met very fully, but the second was not, though our co-workers said they enjoyed meeting each other, in some cases for the first time. This raises some interesting questions (which cannot be addressed in this chapter) about the setting up of, and the factors influencing the success of, support/ consultancy networks for teachers.

Understanding June's View of Reality

June was particularly interesting because of the detail in which she talked about what it was like to be a teacher, and because of her articulation of, and explanations for, the conflicts she experienced with the school organisation. She offered explanations — or theories — for a wide variety of different aspects of her lessons and of her relationships in school. In many instances these theories were implicit in her practices or in her considerations of what actions she should take in particular circumstances. On seeing her actions and those of others on the television, June was moved to try to articulate why she acted in the way that she did. Her comments about how she coped with situations were often descriptive and practical. But underpinning her remarks, there seemed to be an unexpressed schema of theory on which she drew to guide her decisions. In Schon's (1983) terminology, June would seem to be a reflective practitioner whose theory in practice was not fully articulated in formal paradigms and hypotheses, but who, none the less, used conceptualisation and heuristics to guide her decisions and actions.

I have clustered June's explanations into eleven major domains (or field areas) to try to categorise the range of these explanations for the social interactions that took place either within the classroom, or between the classroom and the school, or between the classroom and the wider social environment. I have derived these domains by carrying out a content analysis of all June's utterances during our discussions, but have not sought June's comments upon them. This is for two reasons, one practical and one theoretical. Practically, June and I have lost contact since the academic year 1986/87. She left the school to start a family early in 1988, and I have changed institutions and am now based 60 miles away from her. Theoretically, I would wonder at what point or beyond what point interpretation has to be validated by every participant in the interaction. June did not articulate her thoughts in terms of second order abstractions, but in terms of descriptions of particular events and descriptive statements about her feelings and thoughts on particular events. The abstractions are my attempts to create a conceptual framework to allow me, an outsider, to understand how another person made sense of her work and of the institutional environment in which it took place.

As it is not possible in the space available to comment on all the domains, this chapter looks only at those four in which June described how the culture of the school or the macropolitical environment was linked to the processes of her classroom, and at a fifth in which June explained how she took some of her decisions (see Table 1). These links are particularly interesting. They represent the organisational parameters which circumscribed June's activities in her classroom and challenged her conceptions about being a teacher. There is relatively little research into them, according to Hoyle (1986), and few teachers' explanations for how they effect work in the classroom have been made public. All our co-workers offered explanations for how these environmental factors influenced their classrooms, and expressed fears about extra-institutional pressures upon teachers in the classroom.

The first four domains of Table 1 contain June's explanations for the links between her classroom and the wider environment of school and community:

a. The first domain concerns the interventions of other, usually senior, teachers — senior here meaning either teachers of greater experience, or teachers of higher formal status, or both — as maintainers of the school's organisational cultural norms.

b. The second domain is that of the answerability of the school and of its teachers to the community, both as mediated by the school's senior teachers and as interpreted by the teachers themselves.

c. The third domain is about the expectations and social interactions of the pupils both as maintainers and as subverters of the school culture.

d. The fourth domain is that of teacher reflection and learning to become a teacher.

The fifth domain, a theory of teacher decision-taking, emerges in all the others. The notion of people taking social decisions by using a theory of exchange (carrying out a cost-benefit analysis) is derived from the work of Blau (1964) and of Bacharach & Lawler (1980). Blau (1964) suggested that such theories of exchange, in effect, use economic concepts of opportunity cost to analyse social processes, whether or not people actually use the terminology of economic theory to articulate their thoughts. In interactions that occurred in each of the other domains, June weighed up the conflicting pressures in a situation, evaluated the likely outcomes of applying different strategies in that situation and then took action. This, sometimes, was choosing to do nothing about a problem because she thought the 'costs' of tackling it were greater than either the benefits to be gained from taking positive action or the 'losses' likely to accrue from taking no action.

Interventions of Other Teachers

Before proceeding further, I should explain that the word 'intervention' is preferred to the term 'intrusion' either where there seems to be no clear

TABLE 1 *June's explanations for how the institutional environment influences her classroom, grouped semantically into domains*

Domains	Explanations

How other teachers influence the classroom:	— high status teachers interrupt
	    (a) teacher loses 'face'
	    (b) teacher/pupil mutual sympathy
	— circumstances (time of day; demands of other teachers; rules of school organisation)
	— teacher public documents (reports on pupils; blackboard work)

How the wider environment influences the classroom	— public examinations — (directed) time available — school bus arrangements
How pupils influence the classroom:	— pupil feedback *to* other teachers — pupil feedback *about* other teachers — pupil public activity/visibility

How a teacher learns to be a teacher:	— self-reflection/experience
	— proffered views of other (peer) teachers
	— views of head of department; head of department as role model
	— beliefs about people and how they work including:
	    (a) academic and social needs of pupils
	    (b) involvement in pupil pastoral care

How teachers decide what course of action to take (theory of exchange):	— 'achievement of x is not worth the cost y of effort'

evidence of June resenting another person (usually adult) breaking into the ongoing interaction between herself and her pupils, or where she seemed to accept the incursion as legitimate. Legitimacy here not only refers to a rational-legal framework of an activity being within the job definition of an actor, but also to the perceptions of the person receiving the action that the action falls within the boundaries of shared professional beliefs about what actors might do in particular circumstances. This definition of legitimacy follows the work of Ball (1987) who pointed out that people interact in three different dimensions with the institutions of which they are members: through their professional interests; through their personal interests; and through their personal beliefs. In this case, the term 'professional interests' refers to the job definitions, whilst the term 'personal beliefs' is taken to incorporate people's professional beliefs about what constitutes 'doing a job properly'. June often did seem to resent the interventions in her lessons, but frequently felt powerless to do anything to stop them.

Within the first domain, that of teacher interventions, June commented most explicitly and in greatest detail upon the interventions of senior teachers. Senior teachers intervened in June's classroom both indirectly and directly. Indirectly they intervened through school administrative procedures, such as report writing and class registration sessions. As June pointed out, such procedures limited her autonomy to act in whatever way she preferred and conveyed to her the cultural norms and expectations of the headteacher and his deputies in all manner of aspects of school life. As an example, she explained how she was guided by a head of department in the comments that the school would allow her to write on her pupils' academic reports. These were the reports which were sent to parents — i.e. which formed part of the public presentation of the school to its community.

This ability of a small group of senior teachers to assert its definition of the processes of the organisation more powerfully than other groups and coalitions of participants in the organisation led Thompson (1967) to refer to such groups as the 'dominant coalition'. So when I talk about the views of the school in this chapter, in fact I am talking about the views of this dominant coalition as manifested in official school policy. In this instance of the report writing, the dominant coalition's definition for acceptable teacher behaviour was mediated by a head of department to a junior teacher in order to control how she interacted with the school's community.

Directly, senior teachers intervened in June's classroom for two main reasons: to monitor teacher activity, and to extract pupils. Teacher activity was monitored by direct observation of classroom interaction, as June explained during her stimulated post-lesson discussion:

> I know what people should be doing [in class] because we have senior staff come into our lesson and check on what we're doing. [They] come into our lesson and walk round . . .and they'll look at the [pupils'] books and check on our marking as well' (SRI 07048716).

She pointed out that one senior member of staff had an authorised role to visit teachers' classrooms during lesson time and monitor what teachers and pupils were doing. This is a clear example of senior teachers using the legitimate power of their office — what Bacharach & Lawler (1980) would define as their authority — to gain access to teachers' lessons. In a group discussion in mid-July 1988, our other co-workers expressed great indignation at this infringement of what they saw as the autonomy of a teacher to interact with her pupils in her classroom in whatever way seemed appropriate to helping the pupils to learn. June said that she resented such intrusions, but felt she had to comply with them because of the (higher) status of the teachers visiting her lessons. Lacey (1977) called this form of forced compliance 'strategic compliance', to distinguish it from voluntary compliance. The latter is when somebody chooses to accept constraints placed upon her/his actions because these are perceived by the person as in her/his own best interests.

I suggest that June's objections to these intrusions were at two levels, an ideological level and a practical level. An example of when I see her resentment as being at an ideological level is the following extract. In a post-lesson discussion, June explained:

> I mean it is absolutely appalling. They will just take kids out [of lessons] for any reason. It absolutely infuriates me. Last week in my 'A' level lesson B [a senior teacher] sent for this kid again. And I said, 'well I'm sorry, but he is not going to come out.' Normally I would just let them go and think [that you] don't like to but you have to . But I thought that the lad was doing something important and, 'No! I'm not going to be intimidated.' (PLI.09038704)

She went on to explain that pupils were often extracted for what she described as 'trivial reasons' citing, as one example, how pupils were taken from a fifth-year lower examination class for the whole of a double lesson to put out cups and to make tea for a parents' afternoon. I believe June's resentment came from her perception of a conflict of values between her and senior staff. If the intrusions were the manifestation of the values of senior staff then I see this extract betraying June's belief that teachers, as professional workers, ought to have autonomy in their classrooms to determine how pupils learn.

At a practical level of maintaining control of the classroom, the removal of pupils from her lessons diminished her authority as a teacher with some pupils. June pointed out that some pupils welcomed 'any excuse' to get out of lessons to avoid doing academic work, though she admitted that there were certain pupils whom she did not mind losing from her lessons because they tended to disrupt other pupils' work.

I would argue, following the work of Bacharach & Lawler (1980), that the withdrawal of pupils from June's lessons reduced their dependence on her by making it seem to the pupils that academic work, and the teacher responsible for it, was less important than the administrative tasks, like putting out teacups, and the teacher responsible for these. Further, June's authority to control the pupils during her lessons was shown, starkly, to be limited — she had to comply with the requests of senior teachers. Consequently she lost face in the eyes of the pupils.

The fifth domain, of June's decision-taking, appears in the above account of her refusal of a request by a senior member of staff. She justified her action to herself by making reference to the importance of the task in which the pupil was engaged — studying for 'A' levels — and by which the school and her own performance as a teacher would be judged, weighing this pressure against her expectations of the displeasure of the senior teacher at having his request refused. In deciding what action to take, June used what I would describe as a theory of exchange. As June was aware, the school emphasised high attainment in public examinations by the pupils, a value which one deputy head pointed out to me in an informal conversation. In the light of this, I suggest, June felt able to justify her refusal of the senior teacher's request, both to him and to herself, by appealing to those external environmental demands upon the school (notice her reference in the extract to the public examinations), the validity of which the senior teacher would recognise equally with herself.

Senior teachers made powerful interventions in June's interactions with the school, its pupils and its community, whether directly through monitoring her classroom activities, or indirectly through administrative procedures or through the interpretations of school procedures and norms by heads of department. These conveyed important messages to her about how the organisation expected her, as a teacher, to behave and about what values it expected her to hold — or at least to manifest through her relationships with pupils and other people.

Teacher Answerability to the Community

The second domain is that of the answerability of teachers to parents and to the wider community. 'Answerability' is preferred here to the more usual term 'accountability' since, legally, teachers are accountable to the LEA. June, however, was concerned about her moral responsibility to the pupils and to the pupils' parents and guardians. This distinction follows a threefold typology of teacher accountability which was developed by Barton et al. (1980). The third strand of their typology was professional responsibility. In June's case, her answerability to the community was often mediated by senior staff who, I suggest, based their claim to interpret the views of the community to the staff of the school upon the legal responsibility of the headteacher for the good ordering of the school.

June's sense of answerability had several dimensions, one of which was her concern with pupils' academic performances. Her concern focused on the value of pupils' maximising performances for their own future lives. She did not just want her pupils to achieve reasonable public examination results, but also to learn what she perceived as acceptable attitudes to work. Talking about some pupils whom she saw on her video recording not working hard she said:

> . . . ultimately their exams . . . and they'll just about ruin their chances of that anyway now. But I think it's a bad attitude that they've just got to sit around. I mean obviously when they get to work they'll have the same sort of attitude and I think they ought to expect to do something. Not just sit around. (SRI 070408714)

This concern led June in 1986 to visit a pupil's home, though home visits were, according to her, unusual in her school. As she explained:

> I went to visit one of my pupils because his parents had written in and asked that his work be sent. The head of year said he was not prepared to do it, so I went over to his house (SRI 07048738).

June's concern with pupils' academic performances was paralleled by that of senior staff, though in the latter case, as June's head of department explained, it was to attract the more able pupils from the local primary schools against the competition of other local secondary schools. Consequently June felt doubly impelled to help pupils to achieve as much academic success as possible.

A second dimension was the answerability generated by the geo-social parameters of the catchment area. In her first post-lesson discussion (PLI 020387), June outlined several administrative procedures that the school enacted which constrained her interactions with pupils. For example, pupils were bussed to school, as the catchment area was semi-rural. As a result it was difficult for her to keep pupils in detention after school. She explained that the school's rolling lunch system made it difficult for her to monitor individual pupils' social and academic performance, as pupils whom she wanted to see could be dining at a different time from herself.

The answerability of teachers to the community, and the constraints that this imposed on them (and on June), was often mediated by senior staff. For example the implementation of a rolling lunch system was, itself, a response by senior staff to their fears that the school might get a reputation for ill-disciplined pupils at lunchtime. As June's head of department explained to me:

> The first and second years were on a site down towards M . . ., about a mile away. Then the Authority, under pressure, decided to get us all onto one site. We were appalled by the number of pupils we would have milling around at lunchtime because the catchment area is quite wide. (HODI 04078807)

Consequently, it is difficult in some cases to disentangle how far it was the demands of the community which trammelled June, and how far it was the interpretations by the senior staff of the demands of the community which constrained her. To the extent that June implicitly shared the interpretations of the senior staff — for example, she did not challenge the rationale of the rolling lunch system — it seems a legitimate interpretation to say that June felt herself constrained by her own and the school's perceptions of the answerability of the school to the community.

A third dimension was the sociocultural perspectives of the local community. June did not have much close contact with the community in her capacity as a teacher, so her understandings of the views of the community were largely second-hand. As she explained: '. . . generally policy . . . I don't think you're expected to make contact with the parents at all' (SRI 07048738). To understand how June viewed teaching in her school, then, we have to understand how the senior staff viewed teaching and how their views conflicted with June's. The senior staff believed that the community wanted, above all else, the school to be well-ordered. They thought that teaching was about maintaining order. As one deputy head put it to me, 'we run a tight ship here'. June said that she thought that teaching was about helping pupils to learn by whatever means they could understand and helping people to feel valued (SRI 070487).

One consequence of the emphasis by senior staff on good order was that June had to uphold school rules on pupils' dress. This led her on occasions into a more authoritarian relationship with the pupils than she said she liked. A second consequence was that senior staff tried to regulate the dress of teachers. June recounted the difficulties that she and another young female teacher had had with the headteacher:

> Jenny has recently been told off for her trousers . . . she was taken out of a class and told she wasn't to wear . . . and that she'd been wearing them too much (SRI 07048718).

June, herself, was also asked not to wear trousers.

Curiously, when I asked June whether she thought gender was an issue in her relationships with senior male members of staff, she did not see it as such. She defined the conflict in terms of different understandings about what it meant to be a teacher, even though only one of the senior staff was female.

June's school was not untypical in insulating her (and other non-promoted teachers) from contact with the community, except through formal and transient mechanisms such as parental consultation evenings. Such insulation does, however, give senior staff powerful influence over teachers' practices. As gatekeepers of access to the community and interpreters of community demands to the school organisation, they can legitimate or illegitimate what teachers are doing or want to do by indicating that a particular course of action would or would not be acceptable to the community. Since most teachers in a school are unlikely to have the access of senior staff to the uninterpreted views of the school's community, it is difficult for non-promoted teachers to challenge successfully the views put forward by senior staff.

Pupils as Creators and Mediators of School Cultures

The third domain is the interactions of the pupils both with other teachers and with other pupils. To other teachers, pupils sometimes unintentionally passed on messages about her lessons. As June explained, when commenting on the level of noise she heard during the lesson on her video recording:

> It depends on what I expect of particular pupils . . . on my mood . . . it might be that the headmaster is teaching next door . . . I don't like him to see them getting very disruptive, not that the kids care . . . [but] it's expected that I make them work. (SRI 07048714)

The location of June's classroom was significant in this passing on of unintentional messages. Directly across the corridor was the head of department's room which, like June's, had windows onto the corridor. Unlike her windows, his were largely covered up with displays of pupils' work, making it difficult for a passer-by to see what was going on in his classroom. In addition, one of the heads of year taught in the room next to hers. When teachers walked past her room they could peer in through the windows. On one occasion a wandering head of department, catching a glimpse of a lesson in this way, completely failed to understand it from June's perspective. What June thought was near to disaster he thought was excellent because, as she explained: '[he was] looking for movement but the kids were sat down and I was at the board doing something, and that was a good sign' (SRI 07048719). The disturbance which was upsetting June was a humming by the pupils which, so she said, was not audible through the glass of the corridor windows. By behaving in an apparently acceptable way — sitting down still — the (inaudible) pupils had passed on a message to the itinerant head of department which did not reflect June's perception of reality in the slightest. Another version of this unintentional passing on of messages about teachers and classrooms by pupils, which June reported, was when teachers overheard remarks being made by one pupil to another about life in another teacher's classroom.

June also described how pupils intentionally passed on messages about what went on in teachers' lessons. This had two modes, one of which might be likened to pupils acting as informants, and the other, to pupils acting as spies. The first, informant mode was when pupils proactively told teachers about incidents, and teachers more or less willingly listened. The second reactive mode, of pupil as spy, was when pupils responded to teachers' questions about other teachers' lessons. June described both modes of intentional message-passing in her discussion with me. She disapproved of the proactive mode: 'I don't think it is right to allow [the pupils] to say what they want . . .' (SRI 07048719), and she was incensed at the reactive mode of pupils as spies. She explained how the headteacher had deliberately collected information about her pedagogy from pupils during their career interviews. He had then come to see June and asked her to alter her style of curriculum delivery. June knew of the headteacher's information-gathering because, after the career interviews had finished, one of the pupils had come back into June's lesson and said:

Mr [Headteacher] actually asked me what I actually think about you.
June went on:

I actually complained to the Union rep. about that. I don't think it is right that other teachers ask children about teachers'. (SRI 07048719).

June was acutely aware of the pupils' interactions and said this influenced how she managed her lessons. At one level, she said she was concerned that some pupils' goals were not fully congruent with her (teacher's) goals, and that these pupils could and would subvert her agenda with their own if she did not retain control. For this reason, as she explained, she did not like to see pupils sitting around not working during lessons, even when they had little chance of even a poor grade at the end of the year in their public examinations. 'I suppose the others [pupils] might notice and decide not to work as well' (SRI 07048713). Consequently, she resisted the pupils' agenda when it openly threatened to disrupt her goals. She said that she objected to pupils coming in late to her lessons and then asking other pupils to get out of what they saw as 'their seats' (her words). June insisted that late pupils sat where she put them (LO 090387). As she pointed out: 'I don't want them to think that they can do whatever they want to do' (SRI 07048708). Such findings are in keeping with those of Willis (1977) and Woods (1979) who observed how pupils try to establish control over the activities of teachers.

At another level, June's knowledge of pupils' social networks allowed her to make fine adjustments to the management of her lessons. She explained that she had to stop certain pupils sitting together to minimise disruption in a lesson. At yet another level, her knowledge of individual pupils allowed her to differentiate her reactions to the same behaviour by different pupils. As she said:

> I mean I know mainly which ones are the ones who are going to get it down and which ones aren't. If Paul turns round talking, I know he hasn't got it down. But if James did, then I'd know that he had got it down. (SRI 07048704)

Pupils also influenced June's actions because central to her understanding of being a teacher, as she explained, was her concern for the welfare of her pupils. I suggest that this concern took two forms, an academic form and a pastoral form. The academic aspect is shown by her comments on teaching remedial pupils:

> I use less formal teaching with my remedial class. I've got five and we work all the time on the blackboard or in little groups (SRI 07048720).

With other groups of pupils she admitted to allowing pupils to use whatever mathematical methodology worked for them in solving problems, because she felt the pupils then would be more excited by mathematics and would learn more easily.

The second, pastoral, aspect June showed in her concern for the pupils' social well-being. In 1986 she and four other teachers had set up a Christian Union in the school. She said she had wanted to make pupils feel more valued. As well as having lunchtime meetings, this group also had after-school outings. As a result, June claimed, she came to know some pupils a lot better. She referred particularly to the remedial pupils. This closer contact, as she admitted, altered the relationship which she had with the pupils some of whom, she felt, at one point had begun to take advantage of this to be more ill-disciplined in class. It is interesting to see that June, a secondary school mathematics teacher, described pupils as an important reference point for judging the success of her actions as a teacher. This parallels a finding of Nias (1981) for primary school teachers.

Again, the fifth domain, the theory of exchange, intrudes into this domain of pupil influence on teacher actions. In talking in her stimulated post-lesson discussion about how she decided what actions to take with particular pupils, June explained that she often used a notion of trade-off.

> I can't be bothered to keep telling them when they've got no inclination to do any work for themselves . . . Its just not worth it. Even if I put them by themselves, sometimes they'll just sit and doodle. (SRI 07048712)

The domain of pupil influence on teacher actions is a complex one because it focuses upon an area where two worlds overlap, that of the teacher and that of the pupils. In the classroom, there is a sense in which the teacher is the intruder, intervening in and interrupting the social interactions of the pupils. Elliott (1977) actually referred to the teacher as the 'stranger in the classroom'. Pupils try to minimise teacher interference by enacting their own agendas. Some of these agendas might be to disrupt a teacher's programme; others might be to comply with a teacher's programme, at least in so far as it furthered the pupils' own aims. Yet again, pupils' agendas might be conceived entirely without thought of the teachers. This might be the case when pupils unintentionally give messages to one teacher about the work of another by talking amongst themselves. June said that she did not think that the pupils were bothered whether or not the headteacher heard them chattering during her lessons. It was she who was worried, in case the headteacher formed a negative opinion about her ability to control a class.

If the pupils' world could survive without the existence of the teacher, the teacher's world cannot survive without the existence of the pupils. For June, caring for pupils was the essence of being a teacher. Consequently, pupils influenced June's work as a teacher in every way. At one level, they affected her daily managerial activities in her lessons. June had to decide which pupils to allow to sit together, as well as how to interpret the pupils' actions. How the pupils behaved in the classroom and performed at their work influenced June's relationships with the other teachers in the school. At another level, pupils also influenced June's actions as a teacher through her actively thinking about and involving herself with their pastoral and academic welfare.

Learning to Become a Teacher

The fourth domain is learning about being a teacher in a particular school. Schon (1983) sees practitioners as people who reflect on their past experiences in the light of their current experiences in order to inform their future practices. June said that she did not think the process of learning to adapt to a school as an organisation was a one-way process:

> I don't mind being checked on . . . but I think we ought to have the opportunity to discuss with them [senior teachers] . . . I'd like to justify why something happened or [say] what I was intending at the time when something happened. (SRI 07048718)

She wanted the process to be a dialogue and a negotiation between her, an individual, and the other members of the organisation.

As June explained, learning to be a teacher involved her in learning about the administration of the school, its rules, its rituals and its procedures. In this process she described her head of department playing a central role. She explained how she had, at first, looked to her head of department to help her maintain discipline with her more difficult pupils. In my later discussion with her head of department, he confirmed that he had played such a role during June's early days in the school.

June referred to other teachers, not in a formal position of authority over her, as an important source of learning. In particular she made mention of help she received from other close colleagues who were in her subject area and who were of a similar age and career stage. One such person, she said, was Jenny, a young teacher who joined the mathematics department at the same time as June. It was she who was told off by the headteacher for wearing trousers. In her stimulated post-lesson discussion, June explained how Jenny had helped her to resolve some difficulties she had had in ending lessons.

> I used to really have to finish, sort of fill every minute all the time and yet Jenny, who teaches the same [parallel] class as this, said to me that what she does is . . . And I thought then that perhaps I could be a bit more lenient and give them a reward of a few minutes time [if they had worked well and finished]. (SRI 07048731)

Once again the fifth domain, of teacher decision-making, intrudes. June explained she would like to try group work with several classes:

> Because I think that the kids can gain a lot from each other, that they can help each other. I don't think that a child should sit there and only ask me (SRI 07048722).

But, she said, she had not tried to do so in her non-remedial mathematics classes because she had not learnt how to do so by watching other teachers do it:

> I have never tried the sort of lesson where you have groups working on your normal work [i.e. not special needs pupils]. I haven't seen it in practice . . . so I haven't been prepared to try that yet (SRI 07048721).

I suggest that she decided that she could not evaluate what risks (or costs) were involved in the mechanics of rearranging her classroom. Nor could she determine whether the benefits of small-group work, which she perceived with her small group of remedial pupils, would accrue with larger classes of average and above average pupils. Nor yet again could she decide whether the benefits to pupils' learning would offset the costs to her of reduced class control. Although she said she had seen her head of department make occasional use of group work she did not think this was sufficiently powerful evidence for her to experiment with this form of pedagogy. June did not explain why this was so.

June described another source of learning for her, by referring to her own past experiences, both as a pupil and as a student-teacher. She drew comparison between these and her current situation. She explained that she did not mind pupils making some noise when they were working, so long as the talking was fairly quiet. She said that she thought she had learned this approach to pupil behaviour from when she had been at school in the top stream of a comprehensive school. As she explained: 'We used to get on with our work, but not in silence. But I was in the top band, so I don't know if it was the same in the bottom. But certainly they used to get on' (SRI 07048720). The reference to bottom band pupils was because I had been observing her working with a bottom band mathematics class.

In learning to be a teacher June learned from a variety of sources to adapt to the environment of her organisation. Through her own interpretations of what the school organisation expected of her she became acclimatised to the processes and attitudes of her school. The main sources of her learning were through her accustoming herself to the administrative procedures of the school, and through her interactions with members of staff both senior in status to her and co-equal with herself. Her reflections on what it meant to be a teacher and what she had perceived it to mean in her history, provided her with an anchorage from which to elaborate new interpretations of reality as the environment changed.

Teacher Decision Making

In this chapter I have indicated that the fifth domain intrudes into all the other domains of June's interactions with her social and organisational environment. It seems to be a description of an underlying process whereby June weighed up the benefits of taking particular actions and compared them with the costs the actions would involve, whether they were costs of time, costs of loss of control of pupils, or costs of having to gain more knowledge of either curriculum content or of pedagogical process. After making such an evaluation, June decided what action to take.

June's story seems to offer powerful evidence for the arguments of Homans (1958) and of Blau (1964) that people operate a theory of exchange when taking non-routinised decisions in social situations. This decision-taking can be understood by analogy with economic notions of opportunity cost and cost–benefit analysis. This is important because it begins to help us to understand more clearly the processes by which schools can persuade teachers to make changes in their practices, and by which teachers learn to adapt, more or less successfully, to the institutional environments in which they have to work. In particular it suggests that formal structural models of management are insufficient on their own to explain the organisational processes of schools. A political dimension needs to be incorporated with such models, if they are to describe accurately the processes and interactions which take place between people in schools and between schools and people. Part of this dimension would recognise the importance of teachers being able to trade off their perceived needs and satisfactions against the needs of the school organisation and against the needs of the pupils and their parents or guardians.

Concluding Remarks

In conclusion I wish, firstly, to focus on what it was about June's reflections which made them so interesting and, secondly, to discuss the impact on her reflections of video-recording and of my role as a critical friend.

The breadth of June's thinking and her degree of articulation about her thinking were such as to give me considerable insight into how teachers take decisions and adapt to the environment in which they work. June gave some very clear examples of how she saw her work influenced by the public demands of the wider community upon the school. She also gave clear examples of the political processes by which the internal environment of the school exerted pressure upon her actions in the classroom — through the interventions of senior members of staff; through her interactions with other teachers and pupils; and through the interaction of pupils with other people in and outside the school.

June showed how the school environment exerted pressure upon her practices through her own learning processes. In her learning, she reflected on the demands which the school organisation made upon teachers and upon pupils, and on the messages the school wanted to give to the local community. Her reflections, unremarkably, were second order thoughts about the school as portrayed to her by colleagues with whom she worked. The views of those who worked most closely with her were most influential. In particular, her head of department, in his function as gatekeeper between her immediate world of mathematics teaching and the wider world of the school organisation, was an important purveyor of images. People of her own age and status in the school were other important reference points for June. So, too, were the pupils.

Her adaptation to her school environment was facilitated by her joining a coalition of like-minded teachers about whom we know very little. We do know that the five of them together set up the Christian Union in 1986, so we can presume that they held certain Christian beliefs in common. June suggested that most of these people were also of roughly her age and at roughly the same stage in their careers as she was.

The second aspect has two elements: the impact of using video recordings to help a teacher reflect on her practices; and the part played in that process of reflection by a critical friend. Many of June's more detailed comments and insights into what it meant to be a teacher, and how she has learned about these processes, came when she was watching a video recording of her lesson. This might have been partially a function of environmental factors, such as having more time to talk during the stimulated post-lesson discussion than in the ordinary post-lesson discussion. The only obvious exception to this pattern was when an incident had occurred just prior to my arrival at June's school to observe a lesson and carry out a post-lesson discussion; then, June's reflections on this incident in the post-lesson discussion were as detailed as those in the stimulated post-lesson discussion.

Not only were her comments generally more detailed in the stimulated post-lesson discussions but, in a sense, they were more complex, too. For example, it was in her stimulated post-lesson discussion that June admitted that she possibly derived some of her criteria for evaluating pupil social behaviour from reflecting on and remembering her own experiences as a pupil at school. It was in the same discussion that she elaborated her beliefs about what teaching involved. June's explanations for how she took decisions come, almost exclusively, from her stimulated post-lesson discussion. By comparison, in the ordinary post-lesson discussions, June referred largely to relatively straightforward practical and administrative matters concerning the pupils and the school. This suggests that reflecting on practice whilst watching video recordings of one's practices may, generally, increase the quality and quantity of reflection beyond what might emerge in the course of a post-lesson discussion with a critical friend (often, a self-chosen colleague).

From this research we do not actually know the impact on teachers' thoughts or practices of teachers looking at video recordings of their lessons on their own. We only have evidence of how teachers reflect aloud on their practices when watching video recordings of their lessons with the help of a critical friend, or sometimes, friends. What we do know is that such processes produce very detailed and complex remarks by teachers on how they think about the processes of being a teacher. The importance of the critical friend lies in there being somebody who can ask questions in a non-threatening way to help the practitioner to see the details of her/his practices. Part of being a critical friend is to build up an atmosphere of trust between questioner and reflector. This would suggest that the critical friend is as important to the process of self-reflection as is the process of viewing oneself on a video recording, and that this process of self-reflection is enabled by access to a video recording of one's actions upon which one can reflect with the help of a trusted critical friend.

In presenting this study of June's explanations of her relationships with her school, I have actually presented two studies. One of these is, indeed, about June. Her views can be seen in the transcribed extracts from her discussions with me. Her comments were often made in concrete terms of what people did. Her beliefs and concepts were often implicit in her statements. This raised a problem of research methodology. To facilitate our conversations, early in our contact I had indicated to June that I understood the parameters of an insider's view of a school from my own long experience in comprehensive schools. As a result, I think, June felt it was unnecessary to explicate her views in detail. In our discussions, I found it difficult to keep the balance between pressing her to elaborate her explanations, acting as though my understandings were limited, and allowing our conversations to flow freely.

The second study, that is entangled with June's, is the development of my understanding of her relationships with her school. I had to supply a theoretical framework in which to locate June's statements, in order to appreciate their significance. June did not need to elaborate or articulate such a theoretical framework, I suggest, as she could locate her statements within a practical framework, the framework of her actions. Consequently the analytic framework of this chapter, of the domains and the sub-areas within them and of the explanation for June's decision-making, arise out of my attempts as an outsider to understand her explanations as an insider for her interactions with her school. That June has not agreed this framework, I have mentioned earlier, though neither did she reject it. For the chapter to represent June's conceptualisation of reality, she would have had to agree the analytic framework as well as offer statements of her views on events. I do not claim that the chapter does this; it only reports her views and statements.

This chapter has looked at how one inexperienced teacher explained her interactions with her school and made sense of the reality of being a teacher. In the process, it has also revealed how one inexperienced researcher has tried to make sense of the reality of another person's life in an institution different from his own. It raises as many questions as it addresses, particularly about how teachers learn to adapt to school organisations. But it does suggest that such processes of adaptation involve active participation by teachers, not merely passive induction.

Acknowledgements

The Young Teacher Learning Project was carried out with funding from the School of Education, University of Leeds. Members of the project were Stephen Clarke, Laura Taggart and myself. Stephen Clarke is a lecturer in Education and Laura Taggart is a researcher at the University of Leeds.

References

ADELMAN, C. and YOUNG, E. 1985, The assumptions of educational research: the last twenty years in Great Britain. In M. SHIPMAN (1985), 46–56.

BACHARACH, S. and LAWLER, E. 1980, *Power and Politics in Organisations*. London: Jossey Bass.

BALL, S. 1987, *The Micropolitics of the School*. London: Methuen.

BARNES, J. 1960, *Educational Research for Classroom Teachers*. New York: Putnam.

BARTON, L., BECHER, T., CANNING, T., ERAUT, E. and KNIGHT, J. 1980, Accountability and education. In BUSH *et al.* (1980), 98–120.

BASSEY, M. 1980, Crocodiles eat children. In J. ELLIOTT and D. WHITEHEAD (1980).

BEN-PERETZ, M., BROOME, M., HALKES, R., SWETS, R. and ZETLINGER, B. (eds) 1986, *Advances in Research on Teacher Thinking*. Amsterdam: Swets and Zeitlinger BV.

BERNE, E. 1968, *Games People Play*. Harmondsworth: Penguin.

BEST, R., RIBBINS, P. and JARVIS, C. 1979, Pastoral care: reflections on a research strategy. *British Educational Research Journal* 5 (1), 35–43.

BEST, R., RIBBINS, P., JARVIS, C. and ODDY, D. 1983, *Education and Care*. London: Heinemann.

BETJEMAN, J. 1984, *Summoned by Bells*. London: John Murray.

BIBBY, C. 1966, The evasion of honesty in English education. In A. ROWE (1971).

BLAU, P. 1964, *Exchange and Power in Social Life*. London: Wiley.

BOUD, D., and GRIFFIN, V. (eds) 1987, *Appreciating Adults' Learning*. London: Kogan Page.

BOUD, D. KEOGH, R. and WALKER, D. (eds) 1987, *Reflection: Turning Experience into Learning*. London: Kogan Page.

BOYD, H. and COWAN, J. 1985, A case for self assessment based on recent studies of student learning. *Assessment and Evaluation in Higher Education* 10 (3), 225–35.

BRANDES, D. and GINNIS, P. 1984, *A Guide to Student Centred Learning*. Oxford: Blackwell.

BROCK-UTNE, B. 1980, What is educational research? In J. ELLIOTT and D. WHITEHEAD (1980), 10–14.

BROPHY, J.E. and GOOD, T.L. 1984, *Looking in Class*. London: Harper and Row.

BROWN, L., HENRY, J. and McTAGGART, R. 1982, Action research notes on the National seminar. In J. ELLIOTT and D. WHITEHEAD (1982).

BROWN, S. and McINTYRE, D. 1986, How do teachers think about their craft? In M. BEN-PERETZ *et al.* (1986).

BURGESS, R.G. 1980, Some fieldwork problems in teacher based research. *British Educational Research Journal* 6 (2), 165–73.

—— 1981, Keeping a research diary. *Cambridge Journal of Education* 11 (1), 75–83.

—— (ed.) 1985, *Field Methods in the Study of Education*. Basingstoke: Falmer Press.

BURGESS, T. 1973, Foreword, In C. JENCKS (1973).

BUSH, T., GLATTER, R., GOODEY, J. and RICHES, C. (eds) 1980, *Approaches to School Management*. London: Harper and Row.

BUTCHER, H.J. and PONT, H.B. (eds) 1973, *Educational Research in Britain 3*. London: University of London Press.

CALDERHEAD, J. (ed.) 1987, *Exploring Teachers' Thinking*. London: Cassell Educational.

CARR, W. and KEMMIS, S. 1986, *Becoming Critical*. Basingstoke: Falmer Press.

CHAMBERS, P. 1983, Democratization and pragmatism in educational research. *British Educational Research Journal* 9 (1), 21–25.

CHILD, J. 1984, *Organisation*. London: Harper and Row.

COHEN, L. and MANION, L. 1980, *Research Methods in Education*. London: Croom Helm.

COLLINGWOOD, R. 1978, *An Autobiography*. Oxford: OUP.

COWAN, J. and HARDING, A. 1986, A logical model of curriculum development. *British Journal of Educational Technology* 17 (2).

CROWTHER COMMITTEE 1959, *15–18*. London: HMSO.

CUMMINGS, C. and HUSTLER, D. 1986, Teachers' professional knowledge. In D. HUSTLER *et al.* (1986).

DELAMONT, S. 1980, *Sex Roles and the School*. London: Methuen.

DENZIN, N.K. 1978, *The Research Act*. New York: McGraw Hill.

DES 1985, *Quality in Schools: Evaluation and Appraisal*. London: HMSO.

DESFORGES, C. and McNAMARA, D. 1979, Theory and practice: methodological procedures for the objectification of craft knowledge. *British Journal of Teacher Education* 5 (2), 145–52.

DIAMOND, P. 1988, *Biography as a Tool for Self Understanding*. Paper presented at the University of Surrey, 1988.

DOCKRELL, B. and HAMILTON, D. (eds) 1980, *Rethinking Educational Research*. London: Hodder and Stoughton.

EBBUTT, D. and ELLIOT, J. (eds) 1985, *Issues in Teaching for Understanding*. London: Schools Council/Longman.

ELIOT, T.S. 1973, *Selected Poems*. London: Faber.

ELLIOTT, J. 1977, *The Stranger in the Classroom*. Ford Teaching Project. Cambridge: Cambridge University Institute of Education.

—— 1979, Implementing school based action research: some hypotheses. *Cambridge Journal of Education 9* (1).

—— 1981, *Action Research: A Framework for Self Evaluation in Schools.* TIQL Working Paper No. 1. Cambridge: Cambridge University Institute of Education (Mimeo).

—— 1985, Facilitating action research in schools: some dilemmas. In R.G. BURGESS (1985).

ELLIOTT, J. and ADELMAN, C. 1973a, Inquiry and discovery teaching. *New Era* 54 (9).

—— 1973b, *Innovation in Teaching and Action Research.* Interim report on Ford Teaching Project. Norwich: University of East Anglia.

—— 1976, *Innovation at the Classroom Level: A Case Study of the Ford Teaching Project.* Unit 28, Open University Course E203: Curriculum Design and Development. Milton Keynes: Open University.

ELLIOTT, J. and WHITEHEAD, D. (eds) 1980, *The Theory and Practice of Educational Action Research.* CARN Bulletin No 4. Cambridge: Cambridge University.

—— (eds) 1982, *Action Research into Action Research.* CARN Bulletin No 5. Cambridge: Cambridge University.

ELTON, L. and LAURILLARD, D. 1979, Trends in research on student learning. *Studies in Higher Education* 4 (1).

ENTWHISTLE, N. 1973, The nature of educational research. *Educational Studies: Methods of Enquiry.* Milton Keynes: Open University.

FLANDERS, N. 1970, *Analysing Teacher Behaviour.* Reading: Addison Wesley.

FORWARD, F. 1986, From crisis to prevention: developing a pastoral curriculum. *Pastoral Care in Education* 4 (1), 11–17.

—— 1988, *A Study of the Development of Preventative Pastoral Care in a Secondary School through the Use of Form Based Pastoral Programmes.* Unpublished M. Phil. thesis, Kingston Polytechnic.

FORWARD, R. 1971, *Teaching Together.* Exeter: University of Exeter.

FOSTER, D. 1984, Common sense explanations for the educational development of individuals. Conference Paper, *British Educational Research Association Annual Conference 1984.*

FREIRE, P. 1985, *The Politics of Education.* London: Collier-Macmillan.

GADAMER, H. 1975, *Truth and Method.* London: Sheed and Ward.

GILLIGAN, C. 1987, Woman's place in man's life cycle. In S. HARDING (1987).

GLASER, B.G. and STRAUSS, A.L. 1967, *The Discovery of Grounded Theory.* London: Weidenfeld and Nicolson.

GLASS, G.V. (ed.) 1976, *Evaluation Studies Review Vol. 1.* Beverly Hills, CA: Sage Publications.

GRAHAME, K. 1977, *The Wind in the Willows.* London: Methuen.

GUBA, E.G. (ed.) 1978, Towards a methodology of naturalistic inquiry in educational evaluation. *Monograph 8.* University of California, Center for the Study of Evaluation (Los Angeles).

GURNEY, M. 1988, *The Development of Personal and Social Education through Action Research.* Unpublished Ph.D. thesis, University of Bath.

HANDY, C. 1984, *Taken for Granted: Understanding Schools as Organisations*. York: Longman.

HARDING, S. (ed.) 1987, *Feminism and Methodology*. Milton Keynes: Open University.

HARGREAVES, D. 1982, *The Challenge of the Comprehensive School: Culture, Curriculum and Community*. London: Routledge and Kegan Paul.

HENRY, J. 1986, Towards an understanding of collaborative research in education. In P. HOLLY and D. WHITEHEAD (1986), 86–95.

HMI 1982, *Teaching in Schools: the Content of Initial Training*. London: HMSO.

HOLLY, P. 1984, Action research: a cautionary note. In P. HOLLY and D. WHITEHEAD (1984), 100–103.

HOLLY, P. & WHITEHEAD, D. (eds) 1984, *Action Research in Schools: Getting it into Perspective*. CARN Bulletin No 6. Cambridge: Cambridge University.

—— (eds) 1986, *Collaborative Action Research*. CARN Bulletin No 7. Cambridge: Cambridge University.

HOMANS, G. 1958, Human behaviour as exchange. *American Journal of Sociology* 63 (6).

HOPKINS, D. 1984, Teacher research: back to basics. In P. HOLLY and D. WHITEHEAD (1984), 94–99.

—— 1985, *A Teachers' Guide to Classroom Research*. Milton Keynes: Open University Press.

HOUSE, E. 1977, The logic of evaluative argument. In E.G. GUBA (1978).

—— 1986, *New Directions in Educational Evaluation*. Basingstoke: Falmer Press.

HOYLE, E. 1986, *The Politics of School Management*. Sevenoaks: Hodder and Stoughton.

HUSEN, F. and POSTLETHWAITE, T. (eds), *1985 International Encyclopedia of Education*. Oxford: Pergamon Press.

HUSTLER, D., CASSIDY, T. and CUFF, T. (eds) 1986, *Action Research in Classrooms and Schools*. London: Allen and Unwin.

HUTCHINSON, B. and WHITEHOUSE, P. 1986, Action research, professional competence and school organisation. *British Educational Research Journal* 12 (1), 85–94.

IILLICH, I. 1971, *Deschooling Society*. London: Harper and Row.

ILYENKOV, E. 1977, *Dialectical Logic*. Hereford: Progress Publishers.

JENCKS, C. (ed.) 1973, *Inequality: a reassessment of the effect of family and schooling in America*. New York: Harper.

KEANE, R. 1987, The doubting journey: a learning process of transformation. In D. BOUD and V. GRIFFIN (1987).

KELLY, G. 1955, *The Psychology of Personal Constructs*. New York: Norton.

—— 1969, Autobiography of a theory. In MAHER (1969).

KEMMIS, S. 1985a, Action research and the politics of reflection. In D. BOUD et al. (1987), 139–63.

—— 1985b, Action Research. In F. HUSEN and T. POSTLETHWAITE (1985).

—— 1986, Seven principles for programme evaluation in curriculum development and innovation. In E. HOUSE (1986), 117–40.

KEMMIS, S. and HENRY, C. 1984, *A Point by Point Guide to Action Research for Teachers.* Australia: Deakin University Press.

KEMMIS, S. and McTAGGART, R. 1981, *The Action Research Planner.* Australia: Deakin University Press.

KIRKUP, G. 1986, The feminist evaluator. In E. HOUSE (1986), 68–84.

KITWOOD, T. 1976, Educational research and its standing as science. *Studies in Higher Education* 1 (1).

LACEY, C. 1977, *The Socialisation of Teachers.* London: Methuen.

LARTER, A. 1987, *An Action Research Approach to Classroom Discussion in the Examination Years.* Unpublished M.Phil. Thesis, University of Bath.

LAWTON, DEMMIS et al. 1978, *Theory and Practice of Curriculum Studies,* London: Routledge and Kegan Paul.

LEE, H. *To Kill a Mockingbird.* London: Heinemann.

LEWIN, K. 1946, Action research and minority problems. *Journal of Social Issues 2.*

—— 1948, *Resolving Social Conflicts.* New York: Harper and Row.

LOMAX, P. 1985, Evaluating for course improvement. *Assessment and Evaluation in Higher Education* 10 (3), 254–64.

—— 1986a, Action researchers' action research: a symposium. *Journal of In-Service Education* 13 (1), 42–49.

—— 1986b, Teachers' in-service career patterns. *Research papers in Education* 1 (2), 123–136.

—— 1986c, Course Evaluation as action research. Conference paper, *British Educational Research Association Annual Conference*, 1986.

—— 1987, The political implications of defining relevant INSET. *European Journal of Teacher Education* 10 (2), 221–29.

LOMAX, P. and McLEMAN, P. 1984, The uses and abuses of nominal group technique in course evaluation. *Studies in Higher Education* 9(2), 183–90.

McCUTCHEON, G. 1981, The impact of the insider. In J. NIXON (1981).

McNAMARA, D. 1980, The outsider's arrogance: the failure of outside observers to understand classroom events. *British Educational Research Journal* 6 (2), 113–25.

McNIFF, J. 1988, *Action Research: Principles and Practice.* London: Collier-Macmillan.

MAGOON, A.J. 1977, Constructive approaches in educational research. *Review of Educational Research* 47 (4).

MAHER, H. (ed.) 1969, *Clinical Psychology and Personality: the Selected Papers of George Kelly.* Chichester: Wiley.

MARLAND, M. 1974, *Pastoral Care.* London: Heinemann.

MEAD, M. 1950, *Male and Female.* Harmondsworth: Penguin.

MILNE, A.A. 1958, *The World of Pooh.* London: Methuen.

MITCHELL, P. 1985, A teacher's view of educational research. In M. SHIPMAN (1985), 81–96.

NIAS, J. 1980, Leadership styles and job satisfaction in primary schools. In T. BUSH *et al.* (1980), 255–73.

—— 1981, Commitment and motivation in primary school teachers. *Educational Review* 33(3), 181–90.

NISBETT, J. 1980, Educational research: the state of the art. In B. DOCKRELL and D. HAMILTON (1980).

NIXON, J. (ed.) 1981, *A Teacher's Guide to Action Research*. London: Grant McIntyre.

NOVAK, J.M. 1981, Personal construct psychology and other perceptual pedagogies: an early educational examination and attempt at late Deweyian critique. In M. POPE *et al.* (1983).

OAKLEY, A. 1972, *Sex, Gender and Society*. London: Maurice Temple Smith.

PARLETT, M. and HAMILTON, D. 1976, Evaluation as illumination: a new approach to the study of innovatory programs. In G.V. GLASS (1976).

PATTEN, C. 1986, Address to A.M.M.A. assembly. *Report*. London: A.M.M.A.

PATTON, M. 1980, *Qualitative Evaluation Methods*. California: Sage Publications.

POLANYI, M. 1958, *Personal Knowledge*. London: Routledge and Kegan Paul.

POPE, M., GILBERT, J. and WATTS, M. (eds) 1983, Constructive educational research. Conference Paper. *British Educational Research Association Annual Conference*, 1983.

POPPER, K. 1972, *Objective Knowledge*. Oxford: Oxford University Press.

—— 1976, *Unended Quest*. Glasgow: Fontana.

PRING, R. 1978, Teacher as a researcher. In LAWTON, DEMMIS *et. al.* (1978).

REASON, P. and MARSHALL, J. 1987, Research as personal process. In D. BOUD and V. GRIFFIN (1987).

RIST, R.S. 1977, On the relations among educational research paradigms: from disdain to detente. *Anthropology and Educational Quarterly* 8.

ROGERS, C. 1983, *Freedom to Learn in the 80's*. London: Bobbs-Merrill.

ROWE, A. (ed.) 1971, *The School as a Guidance Community*. Burton on Trent: Pearson Press.

RUDDUCK, J. 1985, Teacher research and research based teacher education. *Journal of Education for Teaching* 11 (3), 281–89.

RUDDUCK, J. and HOPKINS, D. (eds) 1985, *Research as a Basis for Teaching: Readings from the Work of Lawrence Stenhouse*. London: Heinemann.

RUTTER, M., MAUGHAN, B., MORTIMER, P., OUSTON, J. and SMITH, A. 1979, *Fifteen Thousand Hours: Secondary Schools and their Effects on Children*. London: Open Books.

SCHON, D. 1983, *The Reflective Practitioner*. London: Temple Smith Ltd.

SCRIVEN, M. 1967, *The Methodology of Evaluation*. AERA Monograph Series on Curriculum Evaluation. Chicago: Rand McNally.

—— 1986, Evaluation as a paradigm for educational research. In E. HOUSE (1986), 53–67.

SHAKESPEARE, W. 1958, *Hamlet*. London: Methuen.
SHARPE, S. 1976, *Just Like a Girl: How Girls Learn to be Women*. London: Pelican.
SHIPMAN, M. (ed.) 1985, *Educational Research: Principles, Policies and Practices*. Basingstoke: Falmer Press.
SKILBECK, M. 1984, *School Based Curriculum Development*. London: Harper and Row.
SPENDER, D. 1978, *Learning to Lose*. London: Women's Press.
STAKE, R. 1986, An evolutionary view of program improvement. In E. HOUSE (1986).
STANWORTH, M. 1981, *Gender and Schooling*. London: Hutchinson.
STENHOUSE, L. 1973, The humanities curriculum project. In H.J. BUTCHER and H.B. PONT (1973).
—— 1975, *An Introduction to Curriculum Research and Development*. London: Heinemann.
—— 1978, Towards a vernacular humanism. In L. STENHOUSE (1983), 163–77.
—— 1979, Research as a basis for teaching. In J. RUDDUCK and D. HOPKINS (1985).
—— 1981a, What counts as research? *British Journal of Educational Studies* 29 (2).
—— 1981b, Action research and the teacher's responsibility for the educational process. In J. RUDDUCK and D. HOPKINS (1985).
—— 1983, *Authority, Education and Emancipation*. London: Heinemann.
THOMPSON, J. 1967, *Organisation in Action*. Maidenhead: McGraw Hill.
TRIST 1988, *Paper of National Interest*. No 6. TRIST Regional Network, New Approaches for Learning. Sheffield: Manpower Services Commission.
WALKER, R. 1985, *Doing Research*. London: Methuen.
—— 1986, Breaking the grip of print in curriculum research. *Journal of Curriculum Studies* 18 (1), 95–96.
WHITEHEAD, J. 1977, *The Process of Improving Education within Schools*. Unpublished paper.
—— 1980a, The Observation of a Living Contradiction in Education and a Dialectical Methodology for its Investigation. Conference Paper. *British Educational Research Association Annual Conference* 1980.
—— 1980b, In-service education: the knowledge base of educational theory. *British Journal of In-Service Education* 6 (2), 89–92.
—— 1983a, *Teachers' Centres and Action Research*. Paper presented to Gloucestershire LEA.
—— 1983b, The use of personal educational theories in in-service education. *British Journal of In-Service Education* 9 (3), 174–77.
—— 1984, *The Creation and Testing of a Living Form of Educational Theory from Educational Action Research Enquiries*. Paper presented at Kingston Polytechnic Faculty of Education, 29 November 1984.

—— 1985a, What is the logical form of educational knowledge? A question asked within the politics of educational knowledge. Conference Paper, *British Educational Research Association Annual Conference* 1985.

—— 1985b, A dialectician responds to a philosopher who holds an orthodox view of knowledge. *Assessment and Evaluation in Higher Education* 10 (1), 35–52.

—— 1985c, An analysis of an individual's educational development: the basis for personally oriented action research. In M. SHIPMAN (1985).

—— 1986, *Action Research, Educational Theory and the Politics of Educational Knowledge: An Integrated Approach to Professional Development*. University of Bath.

—— 1987a, Inservice education as a collaborative action research. *British Journal of In-service Education* 13 (3), 142–48.

—— 1987b, How can we produce a living educational theory in the context of the politics of educational knowledge? Conference Paper, *British Educational Research Association Annual Conference* 1987.

WHITEHEAD, J. and LOMAX, P. 1987, Action research and the politics of educational knowledge. *British Educational Research Journal* 13 (3), 175–90.

WILLIS, P. 1977, *Learning to Labour*. Farnborough: Saxon House.

WOODS, P. 1977, Stages in interpretive research. *Research Intelligence* 3 (10).

—— 1979, *The Divided School*. London: Routledge and Kegan Paul.

WRIGHT MILLS, C. 1976, *The Sociological Imagination*. Harmondsworth: Penguin.

YEVTUSHENKO, Y. 1962, *Selected Poems*. Harmondsworth: Penguin.

ZEICHNER, K., TABACHNIK, B. and DENSMORE, K. 1987, Individual, institutional and cultural influences on the development of teachers' craft knowledge. In J. CALDERHEAD (1987).

Notes on Contributors

Linda Bannister is headteacher of Walton Leigh School, a special school for children with severe learning difficulties in Surrey. As part of a recently completed school management course at Kingston Polytechnic she conducted an action research investigation of her own role as headteacher.

Pat Broadhead is a lecturer in Primary Education at the University of Leeds. She works with initial training students and as co-ordinator of outstation-based diploma courses for primary teachers. In this book she reports on doctoral research undertaken between 1985 and 1988 as an ESRC-funded student at the University of Sheffield. Prior to this she was a primary teacher working mainly in early years education.

Kate Burton took part in the school management course at Kingston Polytechnic when she was deputy headteacher of West Hill School, a special school in Surrey. She has recently taken up an appointment as an Assistant Education Officer with West Sussex.

Hugh Busher is senior lecturer in education management at Edge Hill College of Higher Education. After teaching in urban comprehensive schools for 14 years he went to the University of Leeds on a temporary contract, before moving to his current post in 1987. His research interests lie mainly in the area of the relationships between individuals and groups in school organisations.

John Cowan is director of the Open University in Scotland. His contribution to this book was written while he was still Professor of Engineering at Heriot Watt University in Edinburgh. He is interested in self- and peer assessment and active learning.

Margaret Follows is acting head an infants school in Croydon. She recently completed the school management course at Kingston Polytechnic.

David Forward is deputy headteacher at Hollyfield School in Surbiton. He has published work on the development and implementation of a pastoral curriculum, which was research supported by Kingston Polytechnic and which led to the award of an M.Phil. In addition to family and church commitments he is a school governor.

Mary Gurney carried out her action research enquiry into ways of developing and improving personal and social education as Head of House at Brockworth Comprehensive School, Gloucestershire. This work has been accepted by Bath University for a Ph.D. and her book *Personal and Social Education: An Integrated Programme* is being published currently.

Barrie Jones is a senior lecturer in Teacher Education at Kingston Polytechnic. For a number of years he has been providing in-service courses where he has helped teachers to develop their guidance and counselling skills. He is currently engaged in a research project involving the collaboration of polytechnic tutors and school-based teacher-tutors in the supervision of postgraduate students on teaching practice.

Andy Larter is an English teacher at a secondary school in Swindon. He has recently been awarded an M.Phil by the University of Bath for his action research.

Rod Linter is Head of Humanities at a secondary school in Surrey. His action research was undertaken as part of the M.Ed. course he is currently taking at Kingston Polytechnic.

Pamela Lomax is a principal lecturer in the Faculty of Education at Kingston Polytechnic. She has published work about girls in secondary schools, in-service teacher education, course evaluation and, more recently, action research. Her present concern is to encourage teachers to use action research as the basis for managing change in schools, particularly change to do with developing staff and increasing school effectiveness. She is a member of the executive council of the British Educational Research Association.

Jack Whitehead is a lecturer at Bath University. He has been supporting teachers in action enquiries for several years now, and has himself published widely in the field of action research. This year he is president of the British Educational Research Association.

Index